Miami Vice

TV Milestones

MIAMI VICE

Steven Sanders

TV MILESTONES SERIES

Wayne State University Press   Detroit

14 13 12 11 10   5 4 3 2 1

Library of Congress Cataloging-in-Publication Data

Sanders, Steven, 1945–
Miami vice / Steven Sanders.
p. cm. — (TV milestones)
Includes bibliographical references and index.
ISBN 978-0-8143-3419-5 (pbk. : alk. paper)
1. Miami vice (television program) I. Title.
PN1992.77.M525S36 2010
791.45'72—dc22
2009050995

∞

To Lynn and Larry
and
The Two Mikes

CONTENTS

ACKNOWLEDGMENTS

Barton Palmer encouraged me to propose a volume on *Miami* ix
Vice for the TV Milestones series. Barton's extensive work on
film has been a model for my own efforts to "cinematize" (his
word) my writing, so I am doubly indebted to him.

No one has helped me more in the work on this book than
Christeen Clemens, who viewed and discussed most of the one
hundred and eleven episodes of *Miami Vice* with me and made
many helpful comments on drafts of the manuscript. We also
worked together to produce the screen captures for the book's
photo illustrations. Christeen and Aeon Skoble, who also read
and commented on several chapters in draft, were invaluable
resources for all things *Vice*-related. Their mastery of the show's
details was an indispensable corrective to my fallible and selective memory. I am grateful to Mark Conard for his comments
on early drafts of chapters 2 and 3, Jim Muller, who provided
insight and guidance, and Jim Trombetta, who corresponded
with me about his experience as a staff writer for the show.

For their knowledge of the city from which *Miami Vice* takes
its name, I have benefited enormously from conversations with
my sister Lynn Lapin, Larry Lapin, Jeffrey Lapin, Gerry Johnson,
Michael Genden, and Michael Stephans, all of whom thought of

Miami as not only a place but also a state of mind. Of course, this book would not have been possible without Herb and Ruth Sanders, who had the foresight to move to Miami in time for me to be born there.

Miami is often written about with an air of condescension. For this reason I am grateful to Dave Barry, Tim Dorsey, Carl Hiaasen, Les Standiford, and Charles Willeford, whose superlative writing and apposite humor provide an alternative basis for understanding what Miami was, is, and will become.

Acquisitions Editor Annie Martin gave Wayne State University Press color and life with her enthusiasm for the project, prompt and informative emails, and unflagging optimism. The comments of the TV Milestones series editors, Barry Keith Grant and Jeannette Sloniowski and two anonymous readers for the press concentrated my mind wonderfully and led to important revisions. Assistant Editorial Manager Carrie Teefey smoothed the way through the production process with her good cheer and encouragement. Assistant Design and Production Manager Maya Rhodes came to my rescue more than once. I thank her for soliciting my thoughts about the book and for producing a look and design that will delight the most discriminating viewer of *Miami Vice*.

I owe a special debt to copyeditor Eric Schramm for his exceptionally close reading of the text and incisive comments. His expertise and generosity with his time led to numerous improvements.

Excerpts from this book, in somewhat different form and significantly revised here, have appeared in *The Philosophy of Neo-Noir*, edited by Mark T. Conard (University Press of Kentucky, 2007) and *Film Noir: The Encyclopedia,* edited by Alain Silver, James Ursini, Elizabeth Ward, and Robert Porfirio (Overlook Press, 2010). I am grateful to the editors and publishers for their permission to reprint.

Vice Inc.

With its instantly recognizable rat-a-tat-tat, rat-a-tat- ▉**1**
tat, rat-a-tat, DUM-dum-dum-dum of Jan Hammer's
Grammy Award–winning "*Miami Vice* Theme," multiple Emmy
and Golden Globe nominations and awards, high-profile cast,
and groundbreaking visual style, *Miami Vice* helped to define
1980s popular culture. As Robert Arnett asks: "Is there a more
iconic image of the mid-1980s than Don Johnson in *Miami
Vice*?" (2006, 127). Perhaps the most concise summary of the
show's undeniable appeal can be found in David Thomson's essential reference work, *The New Biographical Dictionary of Film*:
"*Miami Vice* is . . . full of ideas, often gorgeous, rarely dull, and
hugely influential—not only Miami aped it; TV ads also picked
up on Miami's electric colors" (2004, 575). In this book I discuss *Miami Vice*'s aesthetic appeal as well as its engagement with
issues of personal identity, crisis, and authenticity, and I explain
how the show gives rise to issues of genre, auteurism, and media criticism.

Miami Vice broke with conventions of the cop show drama
in ways that transformed that durable genre into a distinctive form of noir television.[1] As we will see, some of its episodes take the form of realist psychological narratives ("Back

in the World"), some are oneiric transformations of the ordinary into horror ("Shadow in the Dark"), and some are a mix of genres, imperfectly synthesized, perhaps, but with genuine inventiveness in their narratives of urban danger, undercover police work, political corruption, and ethical compromise. Its visual and musical appeal, cultural resonance, and topicality, foregrounding the economic, political, and cultural transformations of the eighties, made it absorbing entertainment in its own day; its exploration of social, moral, political, and philosophical issues also make it worth watching twenty-five years later. The show's shock endings are staples of such successful contemporary series as *The Sopranos, Law & Order: Criminal Intent,* and *CSI: Miami.* At its best, *Miami Vice* is that rarest of things, a text that opened up new ways to experience crime television itself.

2

With *Miami Vice,* television crime drama and film noir coalesced against the dramatic background of Greater Miami to give rise to a TV milestone. With its unprecedented budget of $1.3 million per episode and Michael Mann (*Manhunter, Heat, Collateral, Public Enemies*) at the helm, *Miami Vice* brought feature film production values to prime-time television and became the most recognizable crime show of the decade. Skillfully foregrounding the challenges to Vice Division undercover detectives James "Sonny" Crockett (Don Johnson), Ricardo Tubbs (Philip Michael Thomas), Gina Calabrese (Saundra Santiago), Trudy Joplin (Olivia Brown), Stan Switek (Michael Talbott), and Larry Zito (John Diehl), the show pioneered an uncompromising portrayal of the stresses and excesses of their lives and radically altered the profile of television crime drama.

Miami Vice differed from the television crime dramas that prevailed in the 1970s and was a harbinger of things to come. As David Chase, the creator of *The Sopranos,* told Jim Lehrer in an interview in 2001, "I don't think people cared about the visuals back in the 70s. The first show that I can recall—hour drama—that did care about the visual was *Miami Vice*—I think that made kind of a sea change."[2]

David Chase, creator of *The Sopranos:* "I don't think people cared about the visuals back in the 70s. The first show that I can recall—hour drama—that did care about the visual was *Miami Vice*—I think that made kind of a sea change."

The ambiguous, conflicted aspects of the undercover detective's concealed identity and the permanent possibility of death as a consequence of exposure are indicative of a noir subtext found throughout the show's five seasons. Enigmas of personal identity, encounters with femmes fatales, suspicions about compromised cops and corrupt politicians, and quests for authenticity and redemption—all themes typical of film noir—are among its central preoccupations, never far from the surface in its episodes. The inexplicable and ironic are often found in the details of plot and storyline, and happy endings and facile moral uplift are conspicuously absent. Typical of noir derivations from classic 1940s and 1950s sources, *Miami Vice's* disillusionment is the complete opposite of the attitude found, for example, in *Dragnet*, the hugely popular police procedural of the 1950s and 1960s which, as R. Barton Palmer observes, "mustered considerable rhetorical force in its support of a just society, policed by dispassionate and dedicated public servants, and served by a judiciary that accorded suitable punishment to criminals, thus preserving the rights and property of the law-abiding" (2008, 47).

Miami Vice challenges this cop show convention in which police power is linked with personal rectitude and social justice, questioning whether in our own time the link between them has been broken. The ambiguities inherent in undercover police detective work and the devastating effect it can have are explored in the episode "Heart of Darkness," which I discuss in detail in chapter 1. Other episodes, such as "Golden Triangle," "Red Tape," "Knock Knock . . . Who's There?," "Badge of Dishonor," and "Over the Line," draw out the themes of undercover cops who must convincingly masquerade as criminals without crossing an ambiguous line in a perversion of professional zeal, or who have simply gone wrong. In addition, these episodes show how, even when police officers stay on the right side of the law, they are subject to suspicion. In the pilot episode, "Brother's Keeper," Crockett wonders how Lieutenant Lou Rodriguez (Gregory Sierra) can afford to send his son to an expensive private Catholic school on the pay grade of a lieutenant. Crockett himself falls under suspicion in "One-Eyed Jack," accused of accepting a bribe from Vincent DeMarco (Joe Dallesandro), the right-hand man to gangster Al Lombard (Dennis Farina). In these episodes, *Miami Vice* situates the work of law enforcement in isolation, alienation, and the paranoia of the undercover cops who put their lives on the line each time they begin a new assignment. The series even defied cop show conventions by killing off a main character, Lou Rodriguez, in the fourth episode, "The Return of Calderone, Part 1: The Hit List," reinforcing the mood of danger and paranoia.

Critical and academic engagement with *Miami Vice* begins with a seminal essay by Jeremy G. Butler (1985), still the best article-length study of the show's film noir heritage. Despite one book-length analysis (Trutnau 2005), several dozen book chapters and scholarly articles, and a spate of journalistic coverage, the program remains underappreciated and often misunderstood largely because, in my view, attitudes toward *Miami Vice* are so skewed in favor of its eighties style as spectacle. For example, television studies scholar John Caldwell writes that "MTV and *Miami Vice* certainly were landmark programming developments that changed the way that television looked" (1995, 87). But in his enthusiasm for its undeniable visual style, Caldwell does not mention that the episodes of *Miami Vice* have storylines with both dramatic and philosophic thrust. In addition to discussing the existential themes of alienation, guilt, and authenticity, several chapters of the book bring out the postmodern concern with the lack, or loss, of anything like a personal identity that endures over time. I also discuss the show's serious political and philosophical themes—in particular, the critique of Reagan-era politics and policy that runs through the show's narrative. Close readings of key episodes in each of its seasons are designed to correct the misconception that *Miami Vice* is only about prestige cars, power boats, music videos, and pastel T-shirts.

This book explains *Miami Vice*'s achievement and its landmark status by providing thematic analyses of its storylines and descriptions of the stylized realism that make its episodes unique televisual experiences. Although I approach the show in rough chronological order, I do not hesitate to move freely from one season to another in order to bring together the thematic threads of the show's most compelling episodes and to illustrate its unique contributions. I begin the first chapter with a description of the social, political, and cultural background that led Anthony Yerkovich, the show's creator, and Michael Mann, the executive producer, to use Miami not merely as a backdrop but as a character in its own right. A tourist destination, a once and future film location, and a safe haven for Cuban exiles, Miami is also a locus of the Art Deco, Late Modern, and ver-

5

nacular architecture that provides not one but many cityscapes and makes a major contribution to the show's atmosphere.

I approach *Miami Vice* from the perspective of the revival of film noir exemplified by Mann's feature film debut, *Thief* (1981), with its stunning visual style and protagonist's existential angst. To these elements Mann adds a synthesizer instrumental score by Jan Hammer, a mix of pop tunes (selection and placement by associate producer Frederick Lyle), and a setting in the modernist metropolis of Miami where cops and crooks contend day and night. I include in the first chapter an overview of film noir and describe the central elements of the noir way of looking at the world, a perspective that is fundamental to understanding *Miami Vice*.

My account of the show's role in the transformation of television crime drama into the TV noir of the 1980s and beyond includes detailed discussions of individual episodes, recurring

Atlantis (Arquitectonica, 1982) with its signature sky patio.

themes, and narrative arcs. *Miami Vice* is at the top of its form in its thematizing of suspicion, conflict, skepticism, and irony in four exemplary episodes that I discuss in chapter 2, where I illustrate how these key episodes weave existentialist and postmodern themes into their storylines and style. In chapter 3, I consider authenticity, redemption, and the politics of *Miami Vice* with reference to episodes in the second, third, and fifth seasons, citing the show's attention to the political corruption and intrigue surrounding the war on drugs. I focus on the way the war in Vietnam and events in Nicaragua inflect many of its episodes and are the clearest indications of its prescience and political critique. In this connection, I challenge the view that *Miami Vice* inherently supported the dominant political culture. Rather, I argue that *Miami Vice* has a subversive edge from start to finish.

A central issue to which I turn in chapter 4 is why *Miami Vice* matters. I consider its cinematic photography, innovative use of music, mordant wit, ironic edge, and a social conscience that belies any attempt to dismiss the show as exclusively concerned with surfaces and style. For example, through its broadly based multicultural casting, the show effectively registers, and surmounts, important cultural conflicts. In my conclusion I discuss the 2006 *Miami Vice* feature film written and directed by Michael Mann, and briefly recap the post-*Miami Vice* careers of Mann, Anthony Yerkovich, Dick Wolf, Jan Hammer, Don Johnson, Philip Michael Thomas, and Edward James Olmos.

Three Voices of *Vice*

The viewer appeal of *Miami Vice* has something to do with its initial conception as a drama about undercover cops and crime in South Florida, its music and visual style, and its engrossing storylines. The original idea for *Miami Vice* came from Anthony Yerkovich, an Emmy award-winning writer for *St. Elsewhere* and *Hill Street Blues,* who was developing a movie idea about a pair of vice cops in Miami and was struck by a newspaper item that said nearly one-third of unreported income in the United States originated in or was funneled through South Florida (Sonsky 1989, 5K). Using Miami's pervasive drug trade as background, Yerkovich created a variation on the Miami-as-Casablanca theme.

> I thought of [Miami] as sort of a modern-day American Casablanca. It seemed to be an interesting socioeconomic tidepool: the incredible number of refugees from Central America and Cuba, the already extensive Cuban-American community, and on top of all that the drug trade. There is a fascinating amount of service industries that revolve around the drug trade—money laundering, bail bondsmen, attorneys who service drug smugglers. Miami has become a sort of Barbary Coast of free enterprise gone berserk. (Zoglin 1985, 60)

In another interview, Yerkovich said, "I wanted a city in which the American dream had been distilled into something perverse. . . . I wanted to use the city figuratively and metaphorically. I wanted to place an existential hero in a city based on greed" (Schmalz 1989, A1). With these themes in mind, Yerkovich began to develop a character-driven police drama that would explore the conflicted lives of undercover cops who find it increasingly difficult to distinguish themselves from their criminal adversaries (Sonsky 1989, 5K).

Yerkovich joined up with Kerry McCluggage, an executive at Universal Studios, and pitched the idea for a two-hour pilot to NBC Entertainment president Brandon Tartikoff, who had an idea of his own about how the network might exploit the popularity of music videos. As legend has it, Tartikoff passed the pair a scrap of paper with the words "MTV Cops" written on it. Yerkovich began work on a script, and his would be the first voice of *Miami Vice.*

McCluggage's choice for executive producer of the show was Michael Mann, who had written for *Police Story* (1973–77), *Starsky & Hutch* (1975–79), and *Vega$* (1978–81). Mann was hooked by the script. As he told an interviewer, "It was vivacious, audacious, irreverent. It was something I'd been interested in doing for a long time: pump a contemporary rock and roll sensibility into a *policier* genre" (Harris 1985).[3] Mann was given executive control of the pilot, and Yerkovich's script, called *Gold Coast* at the time, was put in play. Mann thus became the second voice of *Vice* and the one that would come to have predominating influence, most conspicuously through the first two seasons and, as I argue, for the duration of the series. Mann's film *Thief,* starring James Caan as an independent-minded safecracker who gets caught between corrupt cops and the mob, had used visual imagery, film noir lighting, and a score by Tangerine Dream to stunning effect. As others have observed, a zoom in/close-up shot that follows Caan's character's drill bit through a hole in the safe all the way into the lock itself epitomized Mann's technical virtuosity and visual artistry (Meyer 1997, 171; Rybin 2007, 9). *Miami Vice* bears the marks of this auspicious debut and consolidated Mann's reputation as a micromanaging director and executive producer. In a profile for *Rolling Stone,* Emily Benedek wrote, "He is more than thorough, more than inspired. He is obsessed with managing every detail of the show, from script to final edit" (1985, 61). In what others might dismiss as a concern with minutiae, Mann insisted, for example, on placing Bruce Willis's character in the episode "No Exit" (November 9, 1984) in Arquitectonica's postmodern Spear House, quickly nicknamed "Pink House" for its bright pink façade. As the *Miami Herald* architecture critic Beth Dunlop put it, "The Miami that *Vice* producer Michael Mann came to was a place . . . blind to its own virtues. Mann saw its potential: the sharp lines, sensuous curves, bold geometry, whimsical detailing" (1989, 4K).

The same sensibility and obsession with detail that enabled Mann to see the aesthetic qualities of stucco and glass block led *Time* magazine to write, "*Miami Vice* has been filmed under what may be the strangest production edict in TV history: 'No earth tones'" (Zoglin 1985, 60). Don Johnson and Philip Michael Thomas wore clothing by Armani, Versace, and Hugo Boss. Crockett was outfitted in white linen jackets and pink, blue, lavender, or black T-shirts, unbelted linen slacks, and white espadrilles or dark loafers without socks. Mann described Tubbs's wardrobe to *TV Guide*'s Lewis Grossberger as "very urbane, so he has a lot of double-breasted jackets with peaked lapels. A lot of sharp angles around him. A lot of dark shirts with a day-glo purple tie" (1985, 29). Before long, department stores in New York, Los Angeles, and Miami were featuring *Mi-*

Spear House, aka "Pink House" (Arquitectonica, 1976–78).

ami Vice sections. As John Nicolella, the show's Miami-based producer during its first two seasons, told Benedek, "Michael was in charge of the whole visual sense of the show, all this slick stuff—which car, what the clothes look like, the colors, the kind of film cutting. He said, 'It'll be this and this and this,' and he has maintained that all along" (Benedek 1985, 61).

Like Jack Webb, Chris Carter, Dick Wolf, and David Chase—television auteurs who put their distinctive stamps on their highly successful series *Dragnet, The X-Files, Law & Order,* and *The Sopranos,* respectively—Mann created a total atmosphere: visual, sonic, and thematic. Significant aesthetic, narrative, and ideological similarities can be seen between *Miami Vice* and much of Mann's work, including *Thief, Crime Story* (1986–88), a period series set in Chicago and Las Vegas that further extended eighties noir into television, and the feature films *Heat* (1995), *Collateral* (2004), and *Miami Vice* (2006). Mann described his work on *Miami Vice* as like making a movie once a week (Romney 1996, 10), a remark that recalls Jack Webb's description of his intention to make *Dragnet* "a half-hour of motion pictures, not a half-hour of TV films" (Mittell 2004, 143). Richard T. Jameson, the editor of *Film Comment,* expressed the reaction of many when he wrote, "It's hard to forbear saying, every five minutes or so, 'I can't believe this was shot for *television*!'" (1985, 66).

Large historical and cultural events provided background texture and color for the series. Whether examining the atrocities of the Vietnam War and its aftermath or the trauma of Cuban and Haitian émigrés, *Miami Vice* had numerous "noir message" episodes. "Rites of Passage," "Junk Love," "Bought and Paid For," "Streetwise," and "Death and the Lady" shifted the narrative line from the lives of affluent drug dealers, and the mise-en-scène from "color coding and Bauhaus architecture and the Versace spring catalog," in Yerkovich's words (Zoglin 1985, 62), to expose the social ills of prostitution, incest, rape, and pornography.

Nevertheless, it is Crockett and Tubbs's immersion in the demanding business of undercover law enforcement that is used to greatest effect in displaying the drama of their chosen careers. In what is "probably the prototypical *Miami Vice* sequence," according to Thomas Carter (Zoglin 1985, 63), who directed the pilot episode, as Crockett and Tubbs speed across Biscayne Boulevard toward some fateful destination, the reflection of street lights glide off the hood of Crockett's black Ferrari (an effect, incidentally, that can be seen already in *Thief*), and Phil Collins sings "In the Air Tonight" on the sound track. What began as Carter's wish to "use music as psychological subtext" (Zoglin 1985, 63) ends up supplementing the narrative line of the episode remarkably well. And in what *Miami Herald* television critic Steve Sonsky (1989, 1K) called "the most vivid image in a pilot movie full of stylish visuals," Crockett and Tubbs pull off the road and Crockett steps into an illuminated phone booth beneath an electric blue and coral pink neon sign for Bernay's Café and calls his estranged wife to ask: "Caroline, it *was* real, wasn't it?" The whole sequence crystallizes Crockett's sadness over his disintegrating marriage, his isolation, and his fear that he is losing touch with reality because he has learned that his former partner in whom he had put such trust has been providing information about police investigations to the drug dealer Calderone (Zoglin 1985, 62).

In his discussion of *Bullitt* (Peter Yates, 1968), Thomas Leitch observes that "police films feature a hero who is always potentially in danger, so that the dangers of the chase express the dangers implicit in every move the hero makes" (2002, 236). Since Crockett and Tubbs are, by the very nature of undercover work, always at risk, the car chase is emblematic of the dangers implicit in their way of life. Notwithstanding the presence of Carter in the director's chair, the pilot episode's key chase scene reveals Mann's unmistakable influence in its blurring of diegetic and nondiegetic sound. First, all we hear is Jan Hammer's "Chase," an effect that concentrates the viewer's attention on the

Crockett: "Caroline, it *was* real, wasn't it?"

urgency of the moment. Then we hear the sounds of gears shifting as Crockett accelerates, and finally drops of dialogue begin to bleed through, disclosing the officers' desperation to stop the drug kingpin Calderone before he takes flight. When Crockett approaches a red light on Biscayne Boulevard, Tubbs shouts, "Run it!" and Crockett does. The effect of the scene is to remind us of the combative Tubbs and the incorrigible Calderone—the killer of Tubbs's brother—and to emphasize the intensity with which Crockett and Tubbs seek to capture him. The denouement comes moments later at the Chalk's Airline facility as the seaplane that will carry Calderone to safety takes to the skies.

There can be little doubt that Mann's involvement was a significant determinant in shaping the series during its first two seasons. His importance was not limited to his unique visual style but extended to his approach to the whole experience of television crime drama. As Mann noted, however, "I'm very

Despite the best efforts of Crockett and Tubbs, Calderone escapes.

proud of the first two years [of *Miami Vice*]. The content was really out there. But after a couple of years, I don't have the temperament to carry on, I lose interest" (Romney 1986, 10). Yet even after Mann left the day-to-day production details of the show to John Nicolella during the second season to direct *Manhunter* (1986), his influence was so substantial that he did not need to be on the set daily for the pattern of his aesthetic and narrative impulses to be felt.

While Mann was busy with *Manhunter* and *Crime Story*, Dick Wolf, who was writing for *Hill Street Blues* and would go on to be the executive producer of *Law & Order, Law & Order: Criminal Intent,* and *Law & Order: Special Victims Unit,* was brought in as the show runner during *Miami Vice*'s third and fourth seasons. Wolf provided the show with five teleplays and eleven stories, including "When Irish Eyes Are Crying," which he described to an interviewer as "Liam Neeson comes to Miami, Liam Neeson dies in Miami. And what happened in the intervening forty-four minutes was kind of interesting."[4] Wolf's is the third voice of *Vice,* the voice of the linear, highly structured story. During the fifth and last season, which was the show's weakest, producers, directors, writers, and other major creative personnel departed, adding to the difficulty of attaching a single auteur to the series as a whole.

The presence of these three alternative voices in the production of *Miami Vice* problematizes what otherwise might have seemed promising as a straightforward television auteurist approach. As it happens, the account I have given above of Mann's role has itself been contested. As Steven Rybin writes in *The Cinema of Michael Mann:*

15

> Analyzing the television series *Miami Vice,* and connecting its themes and aesthetics to Mann's directorial film work, is especially problematic . . . not only because of the many directors and writers who worked on the series, but also because of the publicly contested nature of its authorship. . . . In interviews with the press certain comments, supposedly made by Mann himself, suggested that many of the series' thematic and aesthetic qualities were Mann's. . . . Mann takes credit for the show's contemporary pop-rock soundtrack. . . . Mann also takes credit for the choice of the Miami setting. (2007, 75)

Even after Mann denied that he had made these comments, which have the effect, if not the intent, of diminishing Yerkovich's role, "Mann still takes a good deal of post-production credit for the *Miami Vice* television series," Rybin writes (76). For example, "Mann claims he was heavily involved in the post-production of every *Vice* episode for the first year and [a] half up until *Manhunter*" (91n3).

Taken as a whole, *Miami Vice,* like any television series, is inevitably the product of the collaborative efforts of many writers, directors, producers, and actors. Given the creative impetus Mann provided during the show's first two seasons, even in his absence while he worked on other projects, the show's complex production ethos was well established, and it may seem reasonable to assume that he was the show's dominant figure. Of course, certain features associated with Mann's visual style or thematic emphases that are important in any analysis of the show's early seasons may not be particularly prominent in later seasons, and for this reason the unexciting but less contentious thesis of the three voices of *Vice* has application because it helps to explain the comparative degree of prominence of these features at different stages of the show's history.

16

Miami, Mon Amour

Among the elements that are relevant to understanding *Miami Vice,* one might list its production history and techniques, the egos and personalities of its creator, executive producer, and principal actors, the network, sponsors, and, more generally, the market context in which prime-time television programming in the United States is produced (Gitlin 1986). One can derive substantial understanding of the show from the work of those who study media in these terms. The same can be said about the work of film and television theorists who provide readings of *Miami Vice* from the perspective of masculinity in crisis (Ross 1986), the privileging of heterosexuality (Wang 1988; Abalos 1999), race, class, and gender hierarchies (King 1990; Deroche and Deroche 1991), and images of law enforcement in film and television (Inciardi and Dee 1987). Nevertheless, my approach to *Miami Vice* is based on the belief that its meaning and appeal can be illuminated by taking seriously both the show's film noir legacy and the thematic preoccupations of Michael Mann. This book is the first brief format monograph to investigate these associations systematically through all five seasons of the series. I have chosen to explore, among other matters, the predicament of characters in *Miami Vice* who must deal with crises of identity, reaffirm their authenticity, or seek redemption as they confront the challenges that come with working as undercover law enforcement officers. My hope is that this study will enable critics, scholars, theorists of the television crime genre, and fans of *Miami Vice* (these groups overlap, of course) to see dimensions of the show they may have overlooked and encourage those who missed the network broadcast of the show and its reruns to discover its riches.

Known as "The Magic City," Miami also has been called "the city of the future" (Allman 1986) and the "city on the edge" (Portes and Stepick 1993). Implicit in these metaphors is the idea of a place that reflects the complex history of late-twentieth-century culture and politics. These conflicting discourses find exemplary expression in *Miami Vice.* By discussing *Miami Vice*'s themes, narratives, visual realization, and sound design in detail, I hope to put readers in a good position to command a clear view of the show's unique contributions and importance.

I grew up in Miami in a neighborhood five minutes from Coral Gables, ten minutes from Coconut Grove, twenty minutes from Key Biscayne, and half an hour from Ocean Drive—all places where portions of episodes of *Miami Vice* were filmed. I mention these points of reference to illustrate that my approach is a thematic and historical engagement with a television show about a place I still think of as home. Re-viewing the episodes of *Miami Vice* is a journey of memory where the shifts of mood, tone, and time remind me that the city, as much as the show itself, is a testimony to change. Perhaps because I witnessed first-hand the efforts to preserve Miami Beach's Art Deco heritage and lived in the shadow of so many icons of Miami's mid-century modern architecture that are no longer extant, I am not surprised when another landmark is bulldozed into oblivion and replaced by a high-rise condominium, a redundant chi-chi restaurant, or a clothing boutique. All of Miami is subject to this fate of displacement and renewal. *Miami Vice* thus is for me a kind of album in which 1980s Miami is encoded on DVDs and removed from jeopardy. I hope this book will have resonance with readers as a compendium of mid-eighties sensibilities and be useful as an analysis of *Miami Vice*'s cultural, dramatic, and philosophical significance.

Sunshine Noir

In the late 1950s and early 1960s, producers, directors, and scriptwriters such as Blake Edwards, Robert Aldrich, and Don Siegel, who had already made important contributions to film and would continue to do so, turned to television to create programs that foregrounded the planning, execution, investigation, and consequences of crime. Classic noir television programs included private detective series (*Peter Gunn* [1958–61], *Johnny Staccato* [1959–60]), urban melodramas (*Naked City* [1958–63]), suspense series (*The Fugitive* [1963–67]), and tales of espionage and foreign intrigue (as in the British import *Danger Man* [1960–62, 1964–66], known in the United States as *Secret Agent*). What these programs made evident is that the thematic elements and styles that grounded the earlier noir novelists and filmmakers were aesthetically viable in the medium of television, which easily accommodated the convoluted and often bizarre plots, urban angst, and cat-and-mouse dialogue of classic film noir.[1]

This period witnessed the development of a trend in site-specific police procedural and private detective television shows. These included *77 Sunset Strip* (1958–64), *Bourbon Street Beat* (1959–60), *Hawaiian Eye* (1959–63), *Surfside Six*

(1960–62), *The Streets of San Francisco* (1972–77), and *Hawaii Five-O* (1968–80). When *Miami Vice* premiered in 1984, the site-specific format returned to television with a noir sensibility that implicated the city as a buzzing hive of criminality and corruption, a place whose disruptive and destructive elements vice detectives Crockett, Tubbs, Calabrese, and Joplin could hardly avoid. (The site-specific format continues to be strong with the *CSI* franchise shows sited in Las Vegas, Miami, and New York, the New York-specific *Law & Order,* and the Miami-based *Burn Notice* and *Dexter.*)

Sonny Crockett's description of Miami as "a place where anything can happen and probably will" offers a working definition of a city that is as prominent as any of the characters in the drama that played out over *Miami Vice*'s five seasons. Long known as a vacation resort, by the 1970s economic collapse made the cities of Miami and Miami Beach vulnerable to ur-

Metropolitan Miami and Biscayne Bay, circa 1989.

ban degeneration and cultural stasis. By the early 1980s, things were even worse. Crime and racial unrest cast a pall over the once vibrant metropolis. In 1984, Dade County reportedly had the highest murder rate in the United States. To this one must add drug smuggling on a massive scale and the intense pressure of the Mariel boatlifts, which brought 125,000 Cubans to Miami's shores in less than six months—people characterized by Fidel Castro in his 1980 May Day Celebration Speech as "the scum of the country" but more accurately described as political dissidents, misfits, mental patients, convicted felons from Castro's prisons, and families in search of freedom and a better life (Portes and Stepick 1993, 21–22).

At the same time, perhaps no other American destination was as passionate about its transformation. With its genius for self-promotion on full display, metropolitan Miami went about remaking itself. Miami Beach, "the place where neon goes to die," in the words of the comic Lenny Bruce, began restoring its Art Deco district and turning it from a seedy, run-down refuge for drug dealers, street thugs, and drifters into a bustling center of social and commercial activity with fashionable clubs, restaurants, and couture boutiques. As real estate developers made speculative investments throughout Miami and its beaches, Anthony Yerkovich and Michael Mann sought out locations, sensing that the quintessentially telegenic Greater Miami would serve as an ideal backdrop to their dramas of the undercover investigations of drug smuggling, arms running, murder, and mayhem. Mann told an interviewer that his first reaction to seeing Miami was "Wow! What fabulous locations! My second reaction was, 'That can't be Miami.' My third reaction was, 'If that really is Miami, let me see more.'" In response to a question about the contested relationship between the actual city of Miami and its televisual reconstruction, Mann said, "The important thing is to create a situation which lets the viewer see what the viewer wants to see" (Allman 1986, 97).[2]

21

Miami Vice premiered on NBC on September 16, 1984, and its success is at least in part due to its approach to episodic crime drama that combined a noir sensibility with South Florida locales and feature-film production values. "Sunshine noir" had arrived, a dramatic exploration of, in the words of Richard Martin, "a daylight world of vice, criminality, explosive violence, universal corruption, paranoia, and psychosis . . . a world populated by corporate gangsters, triumphantly ruthless femmes fatales, psychotic drug dealers and small-time grifters, a fractured world of uncertain relationships and unstable affiliations founded on fear and mutual distrust" (1997, 123).[3] Foregrounding music-directed action, slow motion, handheld sequences, and freeze-frame endings, *Miami Vice* relates stories of drug dealing and smuggling, criminal violence, and political corruption steeped in moral ambiguity.

Music and location make decisive contributions to this updating of the themes, narratives, and visual style of film noir. *Miami Vice* evokes a subtropical climate and waterways where Cigarette, Scarab, and Donzi power boats race and, more often than not, chase each other. The montage sequences following the pre-credits grabber that open every episode and accompany the closing credits represent metropolitan space as a highly colored, brightly lit zone of fast-paced activity with *Cinco de Mayo* parades, grand prix racing, thoroughbred racing, and jai-alai. Many of the most striking outdoor sequences use "magic hour" when the sun rises or sets on the horizon to create glowing tableaux of pink, violet, orange, red, and gold (Arnett 2006, 127). Mann told Sally Bedell Smith of the *New York Times*, "We want to feel electric, and whenever we can, we use pastels that vibrate. When we filmed in the Spear House it was no accident that one of our characters appeared in a pale turquoise shirt against the pink ocher walls" (1985, C20). After several decades of viewing cops in ill-fitting suits driving undistinguished government-issue cars, it is an unexpected pleasure to see Sonny

Crockett in pastel T-shirts and white linen jackets driving what was soon to become a noir television icon, his black Ferrari. *Miami Vice* changed not only the way people looked at television, but also the way they looked at Miami and Miami looked at itself. The city, which had already begun its latest cycle of redevelopment and renewal (to be followed, invariably, by decline, decay, and further repetitions of the cycle), would now proceed to reinvent itself along the lines of the glamorous, style-savvy image that Michael Mann had conceived. Clubs, restaurants, and shops began to take on the designs that reflected the way Mel Bourne, the production designer of the *Miami Vice* pilot, and Robert Lacey Jr., the show's set decorator, dressed their sets.

Architect Morris Lapidus, the creator of those iconic Miami Beach hotels the Fontainebleau, Eden Roc, and Americana, built castles in the sand and put air conditioning in them. Tourists from all over the country flocked to them in search of the American Dream in the 1940s, 1950s, and 1960s. But by the 1980s Miami Beach was a safe haven with trap doors. Mann and Yerkovich found some of those trap doors in a section called South Beach, where the elderly felt imperiled walking the streets after sunset, as if they might fall suddenly into the dangers of drug deals and assaults. *Miami Vice* used South Beach as the site for many of its early episodes, a moment when the area's small, postwar Art Deco apartment houses and residential hotels were being renovated or prepared for demolition, eventually to be replaced by upscale retail shops, trendy clubs, and open air cafes. Yerkovich recalled in an interview: "When we got there, the Art Deco district was somewhat threadbare. Now it's up to its Ray Bans in espresso" (Schmalz 1989, A1). This rapid transformation coincided with the rise of two of Miami's major growth industries, drug dealing and high-fashion photography. The two narcissistic subcultures coalesced in episodes dealing with the sunshine noir of the drug trade and abundant cash. The downside of these changes was that the Social Security retirees and elderly residents of the hotels and apartments along

23

Ocean Drive soon were to be replaced by the models, photographers, and upscale trendsetters who were spreading like a gravy stain across South Florida's Gold Coast table.

In an attempt to capture what he called the spirit or essence of Miami, Mann said, "We take like one-tenth of one percent of the objective reality of Miami and that's what we render" (Sonsky 1989, 1K). This small miracle of editing spliced images of Miami together so painstakingly that only a person sufficiently familiar with the place would recognize how effectively *Miami Vice* links non-contiguous sites and excludes architectural structures and styles too outré for its vision of the city. As Arnett notes, "Miami and Dade County determine the mise-en-scène of *Miami Vice*," and in this respect Mann's creative reinterpretation of reality in his use of the city makes a significant contribution to the development of eighties noir visual style (2006, 127).

A noir television icon.

Music, especially, supports the show's narratives. In a move unprecedented for television at the time, a budget of $10,000 per episode was established to buy the rights to use original pop tunes.[4] Suddenly, viewers were listening to the Rolling Stones, U2, Tina Turner, Eric Clapton, and Peter Gabriel instead of inexpensive covers. Jan Hammer's approach to *Miami Vice*'s score was to do more than merely adapt the expressive possibilities of the synthesizer to each episode's story needs. Rather, his music provides an expansive vocabulary for commentary on themes and characters. In addition to his evocative score, the songs that accompany each episode have such an uncanny fit to the images and actions on the screen that they often serve as functional equivalents of voiceovers. For example, in the pilot episode, Tubbs, new to Miami, knows that the only way he will entrap the drug kingpin Calderone is by calling attention to himself. He goes to a strip bar where he is likely to come to the attention of the dealers who frequent the place. While he gyrates to the music and watches the stripper on the stage dance to Rockwell's song "Somebody's Watching Me," he is indeed being watched—by the bartender who tells FBI agent Scott Wheeler (Bill Smitrovich) that the Jamaican who is making a spectacle of himself and tipping with $100 bills has been in every night looking to score. Another example of music replacing voiceover narration occurs in part 2 of "Calderone's Return," as Crockett and Tubbs speed across the Atlantic to the Bahamas in Crockett's Scarab to find Calderone. The scene is intercut with flashbacks of Calderone's men slaying Tubbs's brother in a drug buy that was a set-up for murder, with Russ Ballard's song "Voices" playing underneath, evoking these memories as Crockett and Tubbs head for a rendezvous with revenge. Other episodes in which music functions as an alternative to voiceover narration include "Little Prince," where Todd Rundgren's psychedelic "Tiny Demons" conveys the subjective experience of getting high, and "Smuggler's Blues," whose title song by Glenn Frey is the leitmotif of the episode. The integration of music and drama in *Miami Vice* has been the subject of much commentary and some criticism, but these musical montages "are not gratuitous or extraneous to the story line," says Yerkovich; they "are designed to contribute to the dramatic narrative" (Smith 1985, 20). Mann says simply that he hopes to evoke "an almost operatic dialectic" (Waters 1985, 67).

Over the course of the series, the demographic, economic, and political transformations taking place not only in South Florida but also in the culture at large are reflected and re-fracted in the lives and fortunes of the show's protagonists. One of its most significant achievements is its ability to connect its episodes with these changes. For example, the aftermath of the war in Vietnam is an explicit point of reference in "Back in the World" and "The Savage" (aka "Duty and Honor"). Interna-tional terrorism is the topic of "When Irish Eyes are Crying." Going from the tragic to the trendy, "The Lost Madonna" indi-

Music as voiceover: chasing Calderone to Russ Ballard's "Voices."

cates how art has become a capital asset and a significant part of drug dealers' investment portfolios. Long a bilingual city, Miami's rapid multiculturalization is due largely to immigration from Cuba, Haiti, and Central America, and so it is woven into the program's storylines. *Miami Vice* registers an awareness of these changes and makes the most of its multicultural setting, cast, and guest stars. Storylines in episodes like the following give but a hint of the show's use of Caribbean, southeast Asian, Chinese, and South American cultural backgrounds: a Haitian crime boss (Clarence Williams III) convinces his followers he has returned from the dead ("Tale of the Goat"), a Santerian priestess (Eartha Kitt) is consulted to develop evidence of the connection between the ritualistic killings of police officers and drug traffickers ("Whatever Works"), a Chilean police officer (Tony Plana) buys cluster bombs from an arms dealer referred by a renegade DEA official ("Baseballs of Death"), a Central American poet (Byrne Piven) is sought by assassins ("Free Verse"), a Chinese drug lord (Keye Luke) comes to Miami to taunt Castillo ("Golden Triangle, Part 2"), an Argentine assassin (Jim Zubiena) has Crockett on his hit list ("Calderone's Return, Part 1: The Hit List"), Yakuza establish a base in Miami ("The Rising Sun of Death"), and, in "Heroes of the Revolution," an East German spy (Jeroen Krabbe) seeks Gina's help to find the man who murdered her mother.

27

In this connection it is particularly important to note the friendship of Crockett and Tubbs. As Douglas Kellner observes, it "presents one of the most striking images of interracial friendship in the history of television" (1995, 244). Michael Mann saw the relationship between the two in aesthetic terms as well, telling an interviewer, "We loved the way a dark star and a blond star played off against each other—visually, it's very exciting" (Allman 1986, 97). Of course, Don Johnson is clearly the center of dramatic interest. This is shown not only in the way the framing consistently privileges Johnson over Philip Michael Thomas and Edward James Olmos, but also in the way camera movement focuses on Johnson, following him when he enters or leaves a room, interacts with the other vice squad members, or interrogates a suspect (Trutnau 2005, 135). Johnson is at the wheel in car and boat chases and plays a dominant role in the choreography of action sequences generally.

A combination of inspired scriptwriting, jaunty direction, and tour de force performances in guest-star roles (by Ed O'Neill, Bruce Willis, William Russ, John Glover, Brian Dennehy, Bruce McGill, and others who now have firmly established Hollywood careers) assured that *Miami Vice* would exhibit a wide range of sharply delineated characters, in addition to its central figures. Character actor Martin Ferrero, in a recurring role as Izzy Moreno, injects fortifying doses of humor, as does Charlie Barnett as Noogie Lamont. Cameo appearances by Ed Lauter, Jeff Fahey, Walter Gotell, and Timothy Carhart, among

Michael Mann: "We loved the way a dark star and a blond star played off against each other."

many others, add texture to the atmosphere. Nearly every episode features quirky, off-center performances. Second leads and character actors (Ray Sharkey, Pepe Serna, Paul Guilfoyle, Lou Diamond Phillips), celebrities (Miles Davis, Bill Russell, Phil Collins, Frank Zappa), stars-in-the-making (Annette Bening, Julia Roberts, David Strathairn, Chris Cooper, Bill Paxton, Laurence Fishburne), and talented newcomers (Steve Buscemi, Larry Joshua, Ned Eisenberg, Kyra Sedgwick) are cast as drug dealers, cops on the take, corrupt politicians, porn performers, con artists, and other shadow figures of the vice underworld.

For much of its first season, *Miami Vice* was scheduled in the highly competitive Friday night slot against *Falcon Crest* (CBS) and *Matt Houston* (ABC). The show placed in the bottom half of the Nielsen ratings even as favorable articles appeared in *Newsweek, Rolling Stone,* and *New York* magazine. In the *New York Times* (January 3, 1985), Sally Bedell Smith called the show "the most talked about dramatic series in the television industry since *Hill Street Blues.*" Summer reruns in 1985 ignited viewer enthusiasm and the show jumped into the Nielsen top ten, where it remained through its second season, starting another cycle of cover stories in *People, Us, TV Guide, Rolling Stone,* and *Time.* Even *Mad* magazine ran a parody of the show. In 1985, *Miami Vice* earned a record fifteen Emmy nominations (compared with the eleven that went to *Hill Street Blues,* commonly regarded as the prestige cop show of the era) and consigned competition such as *Hawaiian Heat* (1984) as well as imitators like CBS's *The Insiders* (1985–86) and *Hollywood Beat* (1985) to early cancellation. Ultimately, *Miami Vice* received nominations for a Golden Globe Award for Best Television Series (Drama) two years in a row (1986 and 1987). Two of its stars, Johnson and Olmos, received Golden Globe Awards in 1986, for Best Performance by an Actor in a Television Series (Drama) and Best Performance by an Actor in a Supporting Role in a Television Series (Drama), respectively. At the 1985 Grammy Awards, Jan Hammer's "*Miami Vice* Theme" received

29

awards for Best Instrumental Composition and Best Pop Instrumental Performance.

Reading *Miami Vice* through Film Noir

The most important influences on *Miami Vice* are not predecessor television police series but those stories of crime and political corruption that entered visual media by way of classic film noir of the forties and fifties and metamorphosed in the sixties, seventies, and eighties into the neo-noir of *Point Blank* (John Boorman, 1967), *The Conversation* (Francis Ford Coppola, 1974), and *Body Heat* (Lawrence Kasdan, 1981). Most critics would agree with R. Barton Palmer that noir films "offer a bleak vision of contemporary life in American cities, which are presented as populated by the amoral, the alienated, the criminally minded, and the helpless" (1994, 6). But it is a matter of controversy whether film noir is best described as a remarkable film cycle that began in the early 1940s and lasted until nearly the end of the 1950s, a distinct visual style with roots in German expressionist cinema, a highly fatalistic sensibility and point of view reflecting American hard-boiled fiction, or all of these. Controversies over how best to characterize film noir have dominated academic discussions for decades and have infiltrated my application of the term "noir" to a subgenre of crime TV generally and *Miami Vice* in particular. In my view, noir television does not constitute a period or movement in the way that the period of classic film noir does. Nor is it simply a programming trend like reality television. Instead, it represents an ever-changing adaptation and extension of the style and themes of its influential film predecessors. Its multiple associations with police procedurals, crime melodramas, private detective series, and psychological thrillers prevent reduction to a single genre.

Like film noir itself, *Miami Vice* is patterned with so many shadings of ambiguity that no single generalization about its meaning is likely to do justice to the complexity, variety, and nuance of its one hundred and eleven episodes. Nevertheless, a sufficient number of episodes support the case that *Miami Vice* is a good example of film noir's adaptation to prime-time crime television, and this is as close as I shall come to proposing a single interpretation of the series as a whole. The metamorphosis of film noir, with its dark portent, enveloping paranoia, and sense of doomed fatefulness, into the South Florida sunshine noir of *Miami Vice* preserves many of classic noir's narrative elements and themes: crime, featuring a contest between good and evil in which the protagonists, as often as not, are seen as antiheroes; betrayal and violence; plot twists and reversals; and a cinematic style (in a departure from the norm, the early seasons of *Miami Vice* were shot on film stock rather than videotape). Even the architecture of metropolitan Miami provides visual correlatives to the show's narratives of deception and disguise in the way walls and facades of glass block conceal more than they reveal.

Some of the most striking images in *Miami Vice* occur in daylight, reversing noir's customary tableau of darkness and shadows and forgoing traditional noir iconography—without, of course, bypassing all visual vestiges of noir. The show has its quota of aerial establishing shots, tilted angles, images of glass, mirrors, stairs, narrow doors and windows, dark enclosures, and the other signifiers of entrapment so distinctive of film noir (Hirsch 1999, 184). But rather than simply reproduce classic noir's urban chiaroscuro, *Miami Vice* showcases South Florida's iconography—the natural, such as Biscayne Bay and the Everglades, and the constructed: I. M. Pei's imposing CenTrust Tower, Arquitectonica's private residence, Spear House, and the Atlantis condominium with its signature sky court on Brickell Avenue. Comparisons of *Miami Vice* with feature films made in Miami during this time, such as *Absence of Malice* (Sydney Pollack, 1981) and *The Mean Season* (Phillip Borsos, 1985), reveal the extent to which the show pioneered a "city on the edge" look.

Consistent with its site-specific format, *Miami Vice* presents alternatives to the low-rent atmospherics of bus and train stations, diners, and cheap hotels associated with classic film noir. Instead, its episodes often depict glossy nightclubs, open air cafes, swimming pools, and power boats traversing the intracoastal waterway. Location shoots include sites known for their beauty, such as Coral Gables, Coconut Grove, Key Biscayne, and the Venetian Islands. But episodes also include downscale sites like the Miami River, The Deuce Club Bar, and the Gayety, a Miami Beach burlesque theater. These low-end venues go against the grain of *Miami Vice's* deceptively stunning South Florida locales and consolidate the image of the debased lives of the drug users, pimps, prostitutes, con artists, shady lawyers, and corrupt officials with whom the Vice Division deals. Jan Hammer's synthesizer score replaced the jazz of classic film noir, while pop, reggae, soul, and new wave singles establish a contemporary mood. With songs like Bryan Ferry's "Slave to Love," "Eyes of a Stranger," by the Payola$, World Party's "Ballad of the Little Man," and Jackson Browne's "Lives in the Balance" directing the viewer's response, *Miami Vice* succeeds at the aural as well as the visual level in creating emotionally significant scenes and leading viewers to a desired reading of the text.

At one level, *Miami Vice* is a show about cops, crime, and corruption, set in "a modern-day Casablanca," as the newsweeklies were inclined to call Miami when the show burst upon the scene. The pre- and post-title sequences of the *Miami Vice* pilot episode counterpoint Tubbs, who wears a suit and trench coat and sits in a parked car on a dark and treacherous New York street, a sawed-off shotgun on his lap as he is about to be confronted by three muggers, with Crockett, who wears linen slacks, a sleeveless turquoise T-shirt under a white linen jacket, and white espadrilles without socks, on Miami Beach's bright, sunny Ocean Drive. A Manichean opposition is thus posited from the outset with the world of darkness ever intruding on the world of light until it is clear that the boundary between them is inherently unstable. So at another level, *Miami Vice* is a meditation on the fundamental themes of the ambiguities of personal identity and the threat of its loss, authenticity and professional responsibility, power relations and political corruption. Events such as the war in Vietnam, the influx of Cuban refugees into Miami, the Reagan administration's prosecution of the war on drugs, and its support of the Contras in Nicaragua are used to establish a framework for both specific episodes and narrative arcs.

Miami Vice's narrative commences in crisis—as Tubbs comes to Miami to avenge his brother's death and Crockett loses his partner, Eddie Rivera (Jimmy Smits), in a drug buy gone

Tubbs in New York City to would-be muggers: "Can it wait? I'm a little busy right now."

wrong—and arcs toward a resolution that will not be reached until the fifth episode ("Calderone's Return, Part 2: Calderone's Demise") when Tubbs's moral conflict and retributive zeal are resolved in a shootout and Calderone is killed. But this is no final resolution because new crises, both professional and personal, arise to drive Crockett and Tubbs deeper into darkness.

Moral ambiguity in *Miami Vice* is typically found in the morally compromised positions of its law enforcement characters, from the police detective who fails to inform the subject he is interrogating of his right to an attorney ("Cool Runnin'" and "Little Prince"), to the undercover detective who is implicated in illegal activity in order to achieve his goal ("Heart of Darkness"), to the police officer whose excessive zeal places an entire police operation in jeopardy ("The Maze"). In *Miami Vice,* law enforcement personnel are sometimes shown using morally questionable measures to gain information, and although these tactics are designed to expose those whose factual guilt is a foregone conclusion, viewers are led to doubt whether their sympathies should lie with the law enforcement official who is carried away by such zeal. In complex cases, conflicting moral and professional obligations, loyalties, and alliances contribute to the sense of ambiguity. For example, in "Give a Little, Take a Little," Crockett is asked in court to name an informant whose life would be put in jeopardy if he were identified as the person whose testimony would land a crime boss in prison. When Crockett refuses, he is sent to jail for contempt of court. In "Better Living through Chemistry," Tubbs's former partner abducts a brilliant chemist who works for the drug dealer Tubbs is investigating. He frames Tubbs for the abduction because Tubbs failed to lie to police authorities investigating a shooting in which this partner was implicated and sent to prison. Now he must decide whether to place Tubbs's life in jeopardy if he is to succeed in obtaining a million dollar ransom for the return of the chemist. These and other episodes suggest that the representatives of law enforcement in *Miami Vice* are likely to be noir antiheroes, on the right side of the law yet just as likely to experience fear, insecurity, doubt, and trauma as their criminal counterparts.

Despite the irreducible residue of moral ambiguity in *Miami Vice*, many of the show's episodes convey moral realism because the drug dealers and smugglers, counterfeiters, home invaders, hit men, and assassins rarely escape or profit from their crimes. Most do not even survive (Skoble 2006, 41–44).[5] What clearly derives from the noir filmmakers and works so effectively in *Miami Vice* is the stamp of individuality in its style and narrative patterns that emphasize life as an arena of conflict and dislocation where alienation, moral ambiguity, and irony are foregrounded.

From the outset *Miami Vice* shatters the audience's expectation of unmitigated success on the part of the police, thereby departing from the genre conventions of earlier police series. The vice detectives are portrayed as all but powerless to stop a rising tide of lawlessness (typically involving drug smuggling but also money laundering, prostitution, counterfeiting, and extortion), in which fellow police officers or federal law enforcement agents are implicated. The show's constant refrain on criminals and those who combat them is that, with few exceptions, there is a fine line between the two, a theme that informs many of Mann's films. This in turn supports the show's political skepticism as the series finale, "Freefall," reveals government corruption so widespread that Crockett and Tubbs resign in disgust. As I argue throughout this book, *Miami Vice* expands the dramatic boundaries of noir television with its emphasis on the jeopardized lives of undercover cops and their search for authenticity. Looking at shows from *Law & Order: Criminal Intent* and *The Sopranos* to *CSI: Miami* and *Burn Notice* confirms how *Miami Vice* explored possibilities that would be further realized in subsequent television crime drama.

The Noir Way of Seeing Things

The interpretive openness of *Miami Vice* is an obstacle to anyone who tries to give a univocal or reductive account of the series, but it also offers commentators and critics the freedom to range widely over the various readings that the show's open texture makes available. This does not mean, interpretively speaking, that anything goes. It is one thing to point to the oneiric aspects of "Shadow in the Dark," "Missing Hours," and "Mirror Image," for example, and another to deny the basic realism of other episodes. Despite the show's openness to interpretation, most episodes of *Miami Vice* incorporate noir's distinctive way of looking at the world, and it will be helpful to indicate five of the most important elements that make up the noir way of seeing things.

First (and for the most part, because there are some notable exceptions), the leading characters in *Miami Vice* are three men whose pasts involve a range of indiscretions, questionable affiliations and motivations, and character flaws. Crockett's Vietnam War experiences and impending divorce, Tubbs's vengeance-motivated impersonation of a New York undercover detective as he seeks out his brother's killer, and the shadowy background of Lieutenant Martin Castillo (Edward James Olmos) as a DEA agent in Southeast Asia illustrate this basic feature of noir male protagonists with troubled pasts. The feature is best illustrated by an episode I discuss in chapter 3, "Out Where the Buses Don't Run," which casts Bruce McGill as a deranged ex-detective whose obsession with bringing to justice a drug dealer whose indictment has been dismissed reveals an unspeakable act from his past.

Second, most of the drama of *Miami Vice* is enacted in the context of a godless world. Events of significance grow out of an impersonal fatefulness or the exercise of human choice rather than from divine providence. The existence of a divine creator and the possibility of an afterlife are rarely, if ever, mentioned either as sources of strength or as solutions to the problems of the central characters. Although religion does not appear to play a determinative role in the lives of any of *Miami Vice*'s seven principal characters, a number of episodes deal with religious themes. "Evan," from the first season, is a meditation on guilt, atonement, and redemption as Evan Freed (William Russ), an undercover ATF agent and former pal of Crockett, must deal with the guilt he feels over taunting a gay fellow officer who subsequently meets his death in a suicidal attempt to disarm his killer. "Whatever Works" and "Tale of the Goat" (in the second season) and "Amen . . . Send Money" (from the fourth season) feature Santeria, voodoo, and feuding televangelists, respectively.

Third, *Miami Vice* is permeated with enigmas of personal identity—its meaning, fragmentation, partial recovery, or ultimate loss. Vice detectives Crockett, Tubbs, Calabrese, and Joplin must maintain a precarious balance between their actual identities and their undercover masks. At its most extreme, a kind of paranoia inhabits *Miami Vice*'s principal characters owing to their need to maintain their undercover identities. Yet even the most outlandish storylines of its paranoid episodes are dramatized in ways that lend themselves to a disconcerting realism and can rise to tragic pitch, as I discuss in chapter 2.

Fourth, while film noir protagonists must make choices and are free in some vague sense, the actions of characters in *Miami Vice* are nevertheless produced and constrained by troubled pasts, an idea reinforced by flashback and other techniques of character exposition and backgrounding. In the pilot episode, Crockett's partner is killed in a car bomb explosion as he attempts to make a routine buy from a drug dealer. Tubbs witnesses the killing of his brother, an undercover police detective, by agents of a drug kingpin. Both events recur in flashback in subsequent episodes. These events, together with subsequent developments that fill out the vice detectives' backstories, lay the foundation for what Butler describes as "the core dilemma of *Miami Vice*": whether Crockett and Tubbs "will surrender themselves to the world of vice" (1985, 296).

Fifth, with few exceptions—the nearly dozen episodes that focus on Calabrese, Joplin, Switek, or Zito—*Miami Vice* frames its narratives on the activities of its three primary male protagonists, and this emphasis on its principal male characters confounds another legacy of classic film noir. The women with whom Crockett, Tubbs, and Castillo have romantic interests are more frequently depicted as victims of drug addiction, shoot-outs, strong-arm tactics by loan sharks, and manipulation by their spouses than as scheming, treacherous villains, as in film noir. The principal female characters are primarily depicted as nurturers, as when Gina Calabrese, with whom Crockett has an intermittent affair, comforts him when he is served his divorce papers and provides emotional support when he is investigated by the Internal Affairs Division. In 1985, it was plausible for Butler to observe that "*Miami Vice* still lacks one key *noir* character: the sexy, duplicitous woman. . . . Surprisingly, all of the women with whom Crockett and Tubbs have become involved have functioned as redeemers" (296). Looked at in retrospect, however, we can see that the episodes "The Great McCarthy" from the first season and "Definitely Miami" from the second offer us chilling examples of the femme fatale type as, respectively, a woman (Maria McDonald) playing Tubbs off against her drug-smuggling boyfriend (William Gray Espy) and a woman (Arielle Dombasle) attempting to manipulate Crockett into a drug deal with her homicidal husband (Ted Nugent). "Little Miss Dangerous" is even darker in its depiction of a psychotic woman, Jackie McSeidan (Fiona), who lures men to their death by killing them during intercourse, a trope that the Sharon Stone character would follow to devastating effect six years later in *Basic Instinct* (Paul Verhoeven, 1992). McSeidan, a young prostitute, misconstrues Tubbs's concern for her welfare as a sign of love, and is devastated when he tries to explain to her that he only wants the opportunity to help her escape from the noxious influence of the Sex World, the nightclub she works at and her base of operations. During an overnight stay at a safe house where Tubbs has taken her in order to get her away from her boyfriend, whom Tubbs mistakenly believes is responsible for the deaths of the men she has recently had sex with, she handcuffs him to a bed and seems ready to shoot him with his own gun when help arrives. (In fact, she turns the gun on herself.) In "French Twist," a seductive French Interpol agent (Lisa Eichhorn) nearly succeeds in killing Crockett when her plan to assassinate a renegade operative backfires, leading Crockett and Tubbs to expose her true mission.

Consistent with its deemphasis on the female principal characters, only a handful of episodes of *Miami Vice* are devoted primarily to Gina or Trudy, including "Blood and Roses," where Gina is raped by the mobster Frank Mosca (Stanley Tucci); "The Dutch Oven," where Trudy discovers an ex-lover's friend is doing business with a drug dealer; "Bought and Paid For," where a Bolivian banker's playboy son rapes Gina's friend; "Heroes of the Revolution," in which Saundra Santiago plays both Gina and Gina's mother, who was murdered in Cuba; and the much-maligned "Missing Hours," the show's notorious UFO episode in which Trudy may have had an encounter with extraterrestrials. Gina Calabrese and Trudy Joplin are virtually always called by their first names, never by their last (as the male principals often are), and are often asked by Crockett or Tubbs to do menial tasks that they don't want to do themselves, such as pulling suspects' files or obtaining records from archives downtown.

Film noir has always been about more than tilted camera angles and chiaroscuro lighting, bizarre plots and urban angst, voiceover narration and flashbacks, though the significance of these elements cannot be denied. The most fatalistic film within the classic noir tradition to observe its protagonist's descent into crisis is *D.O.A.* (Rudolph Mate, 1950), whose doomed accountant, Frank Bigelow (Edmond O'Brien), faces imminent death from luminous poison slipped into his highball at a San Fran-

39

cisco waterfront jazz club; the most extreme and uncompromising is *Kiss Me Deadly* (Robert Aldrich, 1959), in which private eye Mike Hammer (Ralph Meeker) and his secretary Velda (Maxine Cooper) meet an apocalyptic end in the aftermath of an atomic explosion. No one in *Miami Vice* suffers a fate quite as extraordinary as Bigelow's or Hammer's. Virtually every episode in the series reflects modifications and innovations of film noir that were made necessary by changes in both the cultural climate and the medium of television itself. The use of style in the service of content in *Miami Vice* reflects a dedication to the legacy of film noir without overlooking the importance of the storytelling impulse of the program and the constraints of a weekly format. Like the city that gives the program its name, *Miami Vice* is constantly reinventing itself, as can be seen from its significant variations from season to season. For example, in the final season of the series, which I discuss in greater detail in chapter 3, Sonny Crockett's identity has merged with his undercover persona, Sonny Burnett, and Crockett must come face to face with the killer inside him.

Chapter 2

Into the Night

In the first chapter I pointed out that developments in both film and television dating from the 1950s and 1960s provide evidence of the durability and commercial viability of the noir style and point of view. Network television in both the United States and United Kingdom bears the mark of the legacy of film noir with shows such as *Peter Gunn, Johnny Staccato, The Fugitive,* and *Danger Man* that perpetuated the noir tradition with alienated protagonists and classic noir themes such as crime, moral ambivalence, and political corruption. To these *Miami Vice* adds widescreen composition, fast editing, music video–style montages, and such stylistic devices as overhead shots, tilted angles, color analogues of expressionist noir lighting, slow motion, aerial shots, and freeze-frame endings. *Miami Vice* uses a wide variety of visual means to convey the ambiguity of personal identity and the threatening nature of the noir universe. These include nighttime settings and shadows; enclosures, crowded clubs, and bars that convey a claustrophobic atmosphere and suggest entrapment and loss of freedom; dark cars like Crockett's tuxedo black Ferrari; unbalanced framing and composition to suggest awkward or troubled relationships; reflections and mirrors that reveal characters' expressions and the fear and anxiety that motivate them; and foreigners, such as the Cubans, Colombians, Nicaraguans, and Haitians who are often cast as drug dealers and gangsters. *Miami Vice* even has a track-out/zoom-in shot, recalling Hitchcock's *Vertigo* (1958), in the episode "Redemption in Blood" that gives us the visual equivalent of the psychological dislocation of Ernesto "El Gato" Manolo (Jon Polito), Crockett's nemesis in the first episode of the fifth season.

By lending itself to existentialist philosophy and postmodern perspectives, the show expands and enlarges the television cop genre in the process. In this chapter I offer readings of four episodes that illustrate the visual elements, sound design, and narrative means by which *Miami Vice* invests its episodes with philosophical meaning.

Life Lessons and Death Sentences

The absurdity of human existence, the dreadful weight of radical freedom, the permanent possibility of death that sets a limit to one's aspirations and achievements—these traits of the human condition are indicative of an existentialist backdrop and reflect the master theme of the show itself.[1] Consider the alienation Sonny Crockett and Ricardo Tubbs must endure as they live an undercover existence, with its pressures on personal identity and the unresolved conflicts of moral responsibility that arise while they masquerade as denizens of the criminal underworld. The undercover cop must negotiate a world of assumed identities and tenuous loyalties where his or her unmasking is tantamount to death. Michael Mann's frequent characterization of the protagonists in his feature films in existential terms suggests that existentialist readings of *Miami Vice* are rather close to the executive producer's own intentions. The association of *Miami Vice* with themes found in existentialism is therefore not coincidental, for many of its episodes' central characters attempt (and often fail) to achieve personal transformation in an absurd world.

The alienated protagonists of *Miami Vice* take from existentialism a generalized sense of the contingency of things and the ways in which life can go unpredictably off course, as well as a sense of engagement in the name of authenticity and individual freedom. Perhaps this is why in "Evan," an intense noir redemption episode from the first season, the protagonist's last name is "Freed," for this is not only a metaphor for the Sartrean existentialism that sees freedom as the ultimate expression of the human, but also a metaphor for the possibility of authenticity through the exercise of free agency. When Evan, now an ATF agent working undercover, meets up with Crockett again after many years, he is still blaming himself for his harsh reaction when he learned that his and Crockett's police academy buddy, Mike Orgel, is gay. "It was 'faggot' this and 'faggot' that," as Crockett recounts Evan's behavior to Tubbs. Determined not to wind up in professional limbo by being taken off the streets and reassigned to a desk, Orgel confronts a gunman waving a shotgun in public and is killed by a blast to the chest. Evan's subsequent rush toward self-destruction, fueled by guilt and heavy drinking, is postponed long enough for an emotional meeting with Crockett in the vice squad conference room as he breaks down and asks for Crockett's forgiveness. We expect Evan to die by the end of the episode and are not surprised when he throws himself in front of an arms dealer to take a bullet meant for Crockett, thereby redeeming himself at the cost of his own life.[2]

Existential Exit

An episode from *Miami Vice*'s first season bears the title of Jean-Paul Sartre's play *No Exit* and registers an early series engagement with existentialism. Bruce Willis is Tony Amato, an international arms merchant who is negotiating the sale of stolen stinger missiles to Tubbs, posing as Amato's Jamaican connection. This draws the attention of the FBI, as Crockett and Tubbs discover when the bureau threatens to take over their operation. Once the detectives convince the feds that they have already placed listening devices throughout Amato's house and installed taps on his phones, the two law enforcement agencies agree to join forces in a common cause.

Tony's wife, Rita (Katherine Borowitz), is trapped in an abusive marriage and is looking for a way out. Her plight is dramatically illustrated when an enraged Tony pushes her fully clothed into their swimming pool because he thinks, mistakenly, that her dress is not proper attire for a party that calls for formal wear. Rita's repeated pleas for a divorce are met by Tony's insistence: "That will *never happen!*" He even assaults the wife of the divorce lawyer Rita tries to hire and threatens to do the same to the lawyer's child. Eventually Rita attempts to set up a meeting with a hit man in a call that the vice detectives intercept, with Crockett sent to the location of the meet to take his place. At first he gives Rita the opportunity to hire him for the hit, but she declines, saying that although she hates Tony, she cannot bring herself to have him killed. Then Crockett reveals that he is actually a police detective and asks for Rita's cooperation as he and Tubbs work with the FBI to set up a sting operation. Crockett promises Rita that they will put Tony away for good and keep her out of harm's way.

Although the sting is a success and Tony is arrested and taken to court in handcuffs, the pervasive apprehension running through "No Exit" culminates in a memorable closing scene on the steps of the Dade County courthouse in downtown Miami. Officials from yet another federal agency intervene with a court order mandating Tony's release just as Rita arrives on the scene. "You're letting him *go?*" she asks incredulously. The episode seems to be telling us that unless Rita ends Tony's life, there is no exit for her, as we cut to three reaction shots: first, to Tony's startled expression as Rita points a gun at him at point-blank range; then to Rita, who is determined to go through with the shooting; and finally to Crockett lunging at Rita, his look of anguish caught in freeze frame as his cry of "No!" and the sound of the gunshot reverberate on the sound track to close out the episode.

In the Heart of the Heart of Darkness

It was a risky venture to follow the brisk, action-oriented two-hour *Miami Vice* pilot with an episode that achieves almost Conradian bleakness. The aerial establishing shot of a bright and sunny downtown Miami is an ironic comment on the sordid pre-title sequence that opens "Heart of Darkness." Crockett and Tubbs, working undercover as out-of-town theater owners who are in Miami to buy pornography, have been assigned to bring down the operation of South Florida porn impresario Sam Kov-

45

Rita (Katherine Borowitz) at the startling conclusion of "No Exit."

ics (Paul Hecht). On the set of a porn film, the buy is actually a set-up for a pre-arranged bust to establish the pair's credentials as legitimate buyers. ("If all else fails, we can always bust 'em for felony bad dialogue," Crockett quips as they watch a scene being shot.) The ruse works, and they are released from jail in a matter of hours by Kovics's unseen right-hand man, Artie Rollins, who appears to be running interference for Kovics.

Joseph Conrad's short novel "Heart of Darkness" is built up from the long-deferred entrance of its villain, Kurtz. The appearance of Artie Rollins, also delayed, builds enough suspense to suggest that something is not quite right with Kovics's elusive second-in-command. In due course Crockett and Tubbs learn that Artie Rollins is really Arthur Lawson (Ed O'Neill), an FBI agent working undercover in the Kovics organization. A typical neo-noir protagonist, Lawson has immersed himself in his undercover role and has begun to identify with Artie Rollins. He is in fact so caught up in the criminal enterprise he has infiltrated that in a violent sequence, he nearly beats to death a customer who is late with a payment. Crockett and Tubbs also learn that in recent weeks Lawson has cut himself off from the bureau, abandoned the wired apartment in which the bureau had placed him, and moved into a luxurious waterfront condo. He has stopped filing reports and calling his wife; in fact, the first time Crockett and Tubbs come face to face with Lawson, he has a glamorous woman on his arm and introduces her as his "one and only." By now, Lawson's superiors at the bureau suspect that he has gone over to the other side, and these suspicions provide the basis for the otherwise somber episode's running joke: the FBI agents checking up on Lawson are named Doyle and Russo, the Gene Hackman and Roy Scheider characters in *The French Connection* (William Friedkin, 1971).

Lawson is, indeed, a man in the middle, caught between a presumed upright life as a federal officer and a world of sex and money as well as criminal activity in which he participates to maintain his credibility. His aim is to gather enough evidence against Kovics to guarantee an airtight conviction, but while he is undercover he does not want anyone to question his methods. "Are you trying to get me killed? I'm on an investigation here!" he shouts at Crockett and Tubbs after he has learned that they are vice detectives. "If I make a strategic decision to cut corners, to throw the book away, it's my decision, 'cause it's me out here and nobody else," he tells the dismayed pair.

Crockett is determined to use Artie to bring Kovics's operation down, but Tubbs is skeptical about the usefulness of the unpredictable FBI agent. Much of the power of the episode comes from trying to answer questions that arise about Artie's reliability and Crockett's motivation to defend him. One way to interpret the episode, therefore, is to see it in terms of people who have taken on roles and responsibilities that they are neither entirely satisfied in assuming nor feel entirely free

Arthur Lawson (Ed O'Neill) to Crockett and Tubbs: "Are you trying to get me killed? I'm on an investigation here!"

to escape. Lawson wants to give himself over to the satisfaction of desires he has repressed but, on the other hand, he feels an obligation to maintain his role as a respected member of law enforcement. By the episode's end, he realizes that his undercover intrigues have been attempts to give his life meaning, a realization that he expresses when he tells Crockett and Tubbs: "I don't know if I can go back to my wife and that life. It's like I've been riding an adrenaline high, all that money and all those women. And after a while, all of the things that went before, it got like a . . . it's like a . . . I don't know."

The changes that Arthur Lawson undergoes in the ways he feels about his wife and "that life" are manifestations of his ambivalence and anxiety. He seems unable to either reject or wholly accept those drives and desires that are expressed through the persona of Artie Rollins. The roles, relations, and commitments in terms of which Arthur Lawson has defined himself reach back into his past and are not easily forsaken, but the inertial forces of habit and convention that have sustained them are now breaking up as Lawson recognizes he is free to choose how he should live. This realization has estranged him from himself, each side of him at once vying for dominance and constrained by the other.

There is a double realization at the heart of "Heart of Darkness," for Tubbs realizes that Crockett's compassion for Artie has its motivational source in a profound identification with the undercover agent. It reflects Crockett's own ambivalence about the undercover life that he must live in his guise as Sonny Burnett. His role as an undercover detective has produced a tremendous ambivalence, a fear that his alter ego has swept away his real identity as he subordinates his true self to maintain his cover. His role as an undercover agent is no nine-to-five task; its demands encroach on his every waking hour since he must be prepared to act in character at any moment. The constant shift from being prepared to act as a representative of the established order to being prepared to act as Burnett leads to a debilitating and dangerous fragmentation of personality.

When Lieutenant Lou Rodriguez wants to pull Lawson in, Crockett comes to his defense, insisting that they can count on Artie's help. But Tubbs remains skeptical. He tells Crockett, "Artie doesn't know what he's doing from one second to the next. You can't see that right now. You know why? Because you don't see Artie, you see yourself." Nevertheless, in a showdown with Rodriguez, Tubbs sides with Crockett. "Leave Artie on the streets and he'll deliver Kovics," he tells Rodriguez, enacting an oft-repeated bonding motif between the two leads in the series.

A midnight drug deal between Kovics and the vice detectives goes awry and their covers are blown. Kovics, who is unaware that Artie is an FBI agent, orders him to kill the pair, but instead Artie comes to their rescue and then proceeds to execute Kovics and his bodyguard. Motivated by a flawed commitment to the ideals of law enforcement, Lawson knows that he is compromised beyond redemption.

As Lawson is taken downtown for debriefing at local FBI headquarters, George Benson's "This Masquerade" begins on the sound track, extending into the next scene inside the Blue Dolphin Lounge where Crockett and Tubbs are trying to unwind after the evening's harrowing events. The ensuing dialogue foregrounds and underscores the theme of the multiple roles that each of the central figures must play and the subverting of identity entailed by such masquerades. When Crockett admits that for the past three days he has felt like he has been staring at himself in an amusement park mirror that distorts everything out of shape, all Tubbs can say is, "It's not a reflection of you, Sonny. It's the job." Crockett and Tubbs are, of necessity, invested in fabrication, in the presentation of false selves that they must make up in order to survive in the den of sharks they occupy in the course of their work. But Arthur Lawson's masquerade is something more. His casting off of the bourgeois life

49

of the law enforcement officer and his embrace of the fantasy life of Artie Rollins with its sexual enticements has been a flight from an identity that he can neither embrace nor disown.

A disturbing coda consolidates the episode's bleak vision. Crockett and Tubbs are joined in the bar by Rodriquez, who tells them that he has just received a phone call from the federal agent who has been debriefing Lawson for the last three hours: "[Lawson] stepped out for a breather, made a call to his wife, went into the men's room and hung himself." This news is delivered over reaction shots that conclude with Crockett in close-up, his eyes widening in shock, followed by a shot of Crockett, Tubbs, and Rodriguez that ends the episode in freeze frame as the haunting lyric of "This Masquerade" makes its ironic commentary. As an existentialist morality play, "Heart of Darkness" incisively conveys the challenge of living authentically and the high cost of the failure to do so.

Miami Vice and Postmodern Noir

A postmodern reworking of noir is evident in *Miami Vice*: a blending of distinct genres such as film noir, the western, the police procedural, the detective story, and the suspense thriller; a departure from traditional narrative conventions; innovation in the use of sound and music; and an emphasis on self-reflexivity. One can even see the use of Miami as a backdrop to stories of undercover police detectives in terms of irony, with the city's sunshine, fast fun, beautiful women, and handsome men counterpointing an underworld of drug dealers, addicts, murderers, and back-alley hustlers.

In its embrace of popular culture, *Miami Vice* exhibits a postmodern playfulness. For example, in the pilot episode, Crockett and Tubbs set up a buy with Trini DeSoto (Martin Ferrero, who later in the series takes up a recurring role as confidential informant Izzy Moreno), a Cuban refugee and employee of the drug dealer Calderone. By way of small talk, DeSoto tells them that unlike most of the Marielitos stuck in the Miami detention center who killed time waiting for their papers by watching *Family Feud, Hollywood Squares,* and *Ryan's Hope,* he used the time to improve his mind. Tubbs thinks he means that he read a lot of books, but DeSoto sets him straight: "You're missing my point, man. I skip all that network jive, tune in to the old classics: *I Love Lucy, Father Knows Best, Leave It to Beaver, Gilligan's Island.* The Golden Age of TV!"

Before discussing two of *Miami Vice's* postmodern episodes, it is important to call attention to an ongoing debate among television theorists about the postmodern nature of *Miami Vice* and, further, about the nature of postmodernism generally. On one side of the debate, Lawrence Grossberg (1987, 93) writes that "*Miami Vice* . . . is all on the surface. And the surface is nothing but a collection of quotations from our own collective historical debris, a mobile game of Trivia. . . . The narrative is less important than the images." Of course, it could be argued that Grossberg sets up a false alternative here, for why should we deny that *Miami Vice's* striking visual effects and images complement strong narratives? But Grossberg's criticism raises issues that go beyond *Miami Vice's* look. It has application to the very conception of the self, as Douglas Kellner (1995, 238) observes when he writes that "a one-dimensional postmodern reading" of *Miami Vice* (presumably like Grossberg's) leads one to think that the show "is all surface without depth or layered meanings," whereas in actuality "the form, narrative, and images constitute a polysemic text with a multiplicity of possible meanings which require multivalent readings that probe the various layers of the text." A plain way of saying this is that *Miami Vice* can be understood in more than one way and it need not be taken at face value. As Kellner puts it, if one watches the program attentively, one is likely to discover that it "provides many insights into the fragmentation, reconstruction, and fragility of identity in contemporary culture and that it also provides insight into how identities are constructed through the incorporation of subject positions offered for emulation by media culture" (1995, 239). In other words, the show gives us an understanding of what might be called "enigmas of identity" and presents characters who might be models for us to emulate. Grossberg repudiates the idea of the disappearance of a structured, self-reflexive "subject"—postmodernism's preferred term for the "self"—but Kellner argues that the depiction of Crockett and Tubbs as characters who can shift identities as the occasion requires illustrates a postmodern idea that gives depth to the notion of the self, its enigmas and possibilities. If Kellner and others are right, this would support the idea, as I have argued, that postmodern elements infiltrate more than *Miami Vice*'s mood and style. Storyline and theme as well as atmosphere and detail make many episodes of the series work as postmodern noir.

This debate raises theoretical issues that I want to discuss in connection with two episodes that illustrate a postmodern influence at work. In "Shadow in the Dark," narrative is essentially expressive, perspectival, and interpretive rather than descriptive, referential, and objective. The oneiric overdetermination of the episode registers a noir world of new, alternative, and diverse interpretations and perspectives rather than a mirror of nature. The shifting allegiances and paranoia of "Lend Me an Ear" can be understood as indicating postmodern noir's fundamentally indeterminate universe of dislocated values and loyalties ever on the verge of dissolution. In postmodern episodes, conventional values and assumptions are exposed rather than affirmed. In this way, the episodes have a subversive edge, undermining traditional assumptions. Thus, the episodes are postmodern not merely because they use techniques commonly found in postmodern film such as intertextuality, temporal dislocation, and pastiche. Their postmodern character also consists in dramatizing the problematic character of realist assumptions about our knowledge and representation of reality. This has the effect of subverting the conventions of narrative coherence and closure by blurring the distinction between appearance and reality and introducing a destabilizing ambiguity that challenges the possibility of certainty (Thompson 2007, 98).

Of course, the constraints of commercial episodic television and the network structure that sustained them were still too rigid in the mid-1980s to permit anything like the transgressive narratives we now find as a matter of course on cable television if not on prime-time network TV. The episodes of *Miami Vice* that attack bourgeois institutions and convey the message that there is no privileged ethical position or metaphysical subject did so within these constraints.

In a Lonely Place

The ethical irony of "No Exit" and "Heart of Darkness" foreshadows a terror-filled episode from the third season, "Shadow in the Dark," where the theme of existential absurdity gives way to a perspective in which the socially constructed subject is ripe for deconstruction. As we will see, it can also be understood to self-reflexively denote the episode's own narrative processes. The episode brings together the itinerary of the Shadow, the nickname of a demented cat burglar (Vincent Caristi), the instability of police lieutenant Ray Gilmore (Jack Thibeau), who is driven to a breakdown trying to capture him, and the unraveling of Crockett as he tries to pry inside the psychology of the burglar. All this is set in a claustrophobic, nightmarish universe of encounters patterned on the leitmotif of fragmented identities. The dark style is an indication of things to come, as the episode's scriptwriter, Chuck Adamson, would become co-creator of the critically acclaimed two-season series *Crime Story* (1986–88).

The Shadow works an enclave of expensive, multilevel homes with lots of glass. We observe his behavior once he is inside one of them. He covers his face with flour and takes bites out of cuts of raw meat he finds in the refrigerator. He leaves bizarre drawings on the walls. His ragged clothing denotes his status as an outsider, an interloper in the upper-class milieu he is terrorizing. His derangement is so clouded in ambiguity that it is never given hard propositional form but is simply felt. "He's a cat burglar who specializes in pants—no jewels, no hoops, no currency," Gilmore tells the perplexed Crockett and Tubbs when they are commandeered by Burglary Division to help with the investigation. "And he never wakes anyone up." But what is clearly on Gilmore's mind, and increasingly on Crockett's as he enters these proceedings, is what is going to happen when the intruder *does* wake someone up.

Gilmore's obsession with the Shadow has warped his judgment and taken on a life of its own. He is seen questioning a suspect, Wyatt (Timothy Carhart), who is confined to a wheel-

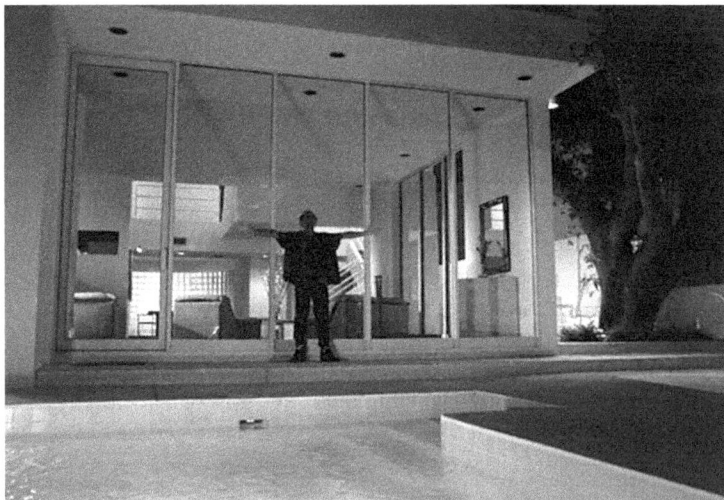

The Shadow (Vincent Caristi) works an enclave of multilevel houses with lots of glass.

chair. Gilmore suddenly dumps Wyatt onto the pavement when he doesn't answer questions to Gilmore's satisfaction. Before long, Gilmore himself is found in the kitchen of a home where he believes he has cornered the intruder. He fires his weapon at the freezer unit where he insists the Shadow is hiding. When police officers arrive on the scene to take him into custody, he is babbling: "To catch these guys you gotta think like 'em, feel like 'em, walk like 'em, talk like 'em, see like 'em . . ."

As Crockett is drawn deeper into the investigation, there is a stylish delirium to his own fascination with the Shadow. He tries to decode the intruder's malevolent pattern by circumventing normal investigative procedures and putting himself into the Shadow's mindset. "Shadow in the Dark" is given a look that echoes and comments on these disorienting and disturbing aspects of Crockett's behavior, as in the scene in which Crockett

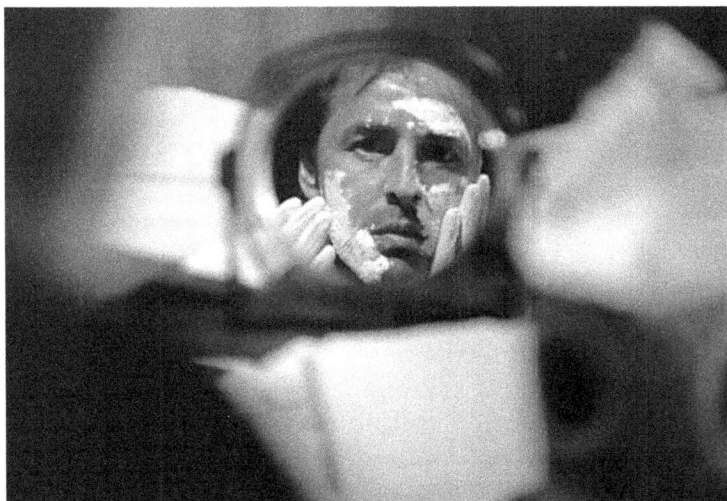

A stylish delirium to Crockett's fascination with the Shadow.

stares into a mirror and applies flour to his own face as he attempts to mimic the cat burglar's persona.

Crockett photographs houses in the city's northeast grid and tries to pick out the site of the next home invasion. "There's something about these houses . . . certain kinds of houses, a certain vibe. There's something about these drawings, Gilmore was cueing in on them. I can't explain," he tells Castillo, "but I think I'm on to it." He patrols the area at night in a scene in which deep blacks predominate, as in much of film noir. In a riveting sequence, he sees the bizarre drawings of the intruder on a neighborhood sidewalk and enters a backyard in search of him. In a series of quick cuts shot from low angles, the intruder comes at Crockett at close range with a startling, high-pitched screech, followed by another quick cut to Crockett at his desk at headquarters as he abruptly wakes from this nightmare, knocking over a lamp. This fast cutting is followed by a slower-paced sequence as Crockett calls in Tubbs, Switek, Gina, and Trudy for an impromptu midnight search of the neighborhood where he has just "seen" the intruder in his dream. They find nothing, even as we see the intruder lurking in the darkness as Crockett and Tubbs drive away. Later in the episode the effect of this stunning bit of foreshadowing will be fully revealed.

The investigation begins to take its toll on Crockett. Everything from the night-for-night photography to Jan Hammer's eerie score serves to externalize Crockett's mental state, which starts out as a laconic foreboding and rapidly deteriorates into dread. Castillo finds him having an after-dinner drink as the early morning sun pours through the window of a street-front cafe. Castillo orders two cups of coffee but Crockett signals to the waiter for another shot instead. Castillo tells his detective to just "think straight," but Crockett insists that he doesn't need to think straight, he needs to think like the Shadow. "The answer we need is not in the book, it's in his head," he tells the dubious Castillo.

Vice turns up empty-handed on Crockett's hunch about where to find the Shadow.

Typical of postmodern noir derivations from classic sources, "Shadow in the Dark" conveys a chilling portrait of a criminal whose violence is pointless and therefore inexplicable by conventional means. The illusory and dream-like aspects of the episode externalize Crockett's realization that he cannot catch the Shadow by ordinary criminal investigative means. The portion of the episode that functions as a police procedural is thus especially compelling because by deliberately foregrounding the criminal investigative process, the episode dramatizes the difficulty of distinguishing appearance from reality in the postmodern noir universe. By a process of reenacting the mental life of the Shadow, Crockett has an insight into the location of the next home invasion, and in a one-on-one encounter with his former adversary Gilmore, now confined to a psychiatric lockup, Crockett is able to confirm this insight.

Once Crockett has achieved this understanding, he manages to trap the Shadow in the process of a break-in, knife in hand as he is about to confront his victim. Crockett beats the man bloody before officers arrive on the scene to take the Shadow into custody. But the effect that he has had on Crockett is palpable. He taunts the vice detective as he is led away by police: "You live with me, don't you?"

"Shadow in the Dark" is not only an account of Crockett's unrelenting search through a dark world to find a demented intruder. It is also Crockett's interrogation of himself. When the suspect is being given a polygraph examination, Crockett sits on the observer's side of a two-way mirror, and, for a moment, we have a side-view of both men. As we cut to Crockett's point of view, we see and hear the prisoner's non-sequitur responses

through the plate glass partition that gives Crockett a view into the examination room. Throughout the episode, references to and images of glass predominate. The intent seems to be to reveal the dislocations and distortions that all attempts to interrogate or discover the truth impose on their subject-matter, and to disavow once and for all the realist assumption that the camera gives us reality as if shot through a pane of glass.[3] If anything, these sequences are emblematic of the failure and perhaps the impossibility of getting at the truth.

A close-up shot of the intruder's face as reflected in the glass window that separates him from Crockett is followed by a quick cut as the man suddenly smashes the glass, then by another quick cut to Crockett the moment he wakes up in confusion on board his sloop the *St. Vitus Dance,* echoing the end of the earlier nightmare sequence. This abrupt transition undermines our confidence in Crockett's ability to distinguish dream from reality, a reversal of conventional narrative assumptions that is the most destabilizing feature of the episode. The ending strongly suggests that what we have been witnessing has all been Crockett's dream. If it has not been his dream, we are left to wonder at what cost Crockett has purchased his triumph.

The price of his victory is bound to be many nights of troubled sleep. We fade out on Crockett, face in hands, trying to rub from his head the terror of it all.

Ironically, "Shadow in the Dark" succeeds in telling the story it wants to tell even as it subverts conventional narrative. The very title is ironic because there can be no shadow without a source of light, and it is the light that Crockett is intent on finding. The episode is also unconventional in offering no final resolution. Instead, it closes with a deliberate distancing effect, keeping us in suspense and making us observers of and participants in Crockett's confusion while calling into question the reliability of what we have been shown all along. With the episode's dreamlike confusion, "Shadow in the Dark" ends on an ambiguous note.

59

Paranoia and Real Enemies

In "Heart of Darkness," self-identity is built upon a fantasy life to which the FBI agent Arthur Lawson is so drawn that he is finally consumed by it. "Shadow in the Dark" depicts an implosion of the self on itself. But fantasy and isolation are not the only sources of jeopardy to the self. There is also a potent element in both classic noir and the postmodern noir variations that followed: paranoid fear, with its obvious potential for cognitive impairment and emotional fracture.

"Lend Me an Ear" opens with an exterior sequence as a seaplane descends from the clouds and sets down in Biscayne Bay. Crockett and Tubbs watch from a distance, hoping they will see Alexander Dykstra (Yorgo Voyagis) off-load drugs onto a speedboat docked alongside the seaplane. As the boat speeds away with someone else at the wheel, they give chase through a narrow waterway running parallel to the highway until the driver attempts a sharp turn. The boat then hydroplanes and goes flying into the air, coming down on the road, sliding across four lanes, and screeching to a halt at the curb. The driver is dead. "Neck snapped" is Crockett's quick diagnosis at the scene. But there is no trace of Dykstra or the drugs they thought they would find on the boat. In fact, as we eventually discover, Dykstra is not importing drugs at all. In the guise of helping the drug dealers send their cash out of the country, Dykstra is killing them and keeping their profits for himself.

The vice squad rents high-tech bugging devices from ex-cop and electronics expert Steve Duddy (John Glover) so they can conduct surveillance of Dykstra. Duddy's is a noir world because it is morally ambiguous. His opportunism plays no favorites. In fact, he also conducts lucrative "defensive sweeping" for Dykstra himself. When he discovers the rented bugs inside Dykstra's house and realizes that Dykstra is the target of vice's investigation, he keeps this conflict of interest to himself. Duddy's topsy-turvy moral perspective is nicely conveyed by a striking 180-degree angled shot of Dykstra's staircase that Duddy is descending, debugging equipment in hand as he sweeps Dykstra's posh home.

The inevitable collision comes when Duddy witnesses Dykstra interrogating his girlfriend with Duddy's own voice-stress analyzer. Dykstra catches her in a lie and shoots her dead. "I cannot tolerate dishonesty," he tells the stunned electronics wizard. Duddy reports the murder by placing an anonymous phone call to the police. The tape of the call is sent to Crockett and Tubbs, who, in turn, take it to Duddy for analysis. "This voice has been electronically altered," he tells them. "No way you're going to get a voice print. Why don't you just pick him up? You've got your tip." In exasperated tones they complain that they have no evidence with which to charge Dykstra.

In order to help the vice detectives ensnare Dykstra, Duddy prepares an edited tape based on surreptitiously recorded telephone conversations of Dykstra's that are innocuous in themselves but devastating in the doctored version, in which it appears that he has revealed his entire operation to McGregor, his most recent client (and victim). The irony is that Dykstra actually has done the things discussed on the doctored tape, but there is no way the vice detectives can know this. Duddy thus feeds them what they initially assume is evidence from Dykstra's own mouth that they can use to arrest him.

Crockett sees through Duddy's manipulations when he discovers a fatal discrepancy between the time McGregor was killed and the time the incriminating conversation with him was supposed to have taken place. He and Tubbs converge on Duddy's house, but not before Dykstra and his gunmen have arrived. Anticipating Dykstra's discovery of the burst transmitters he has used to bug his home, Duddy is waiting for him. He distracts Dykstra with a video of himself on his big screen television holding a gun and shouting, "Even paranoids have real enemies!" and shoots him dead. Crockett promptly arrests Duddy, but the district attorney refuses to press charges. Crockett is furious but Castillo makes it clear that he is not going to challenge the DA's decision.

The precursors of "Lend Me an Ear" are the paranoid thrillers of the early 1970s such as *The Anderson Tapes* (Sidney Lumet, 1971), *The Parallax View* (Alan J. Pakula, 1974), and *The Conversation* (Francis Ford Coppola, 1974), whose protagonists—played by Sean Connery, Warren Beatty, and Gene Hackman, respectively—are suspicious even when they are unaware of the extent to which their suspicions reflect the existence of real enemies. In a remarkable set-piece reminiscent of *The Conversation,* a film that "Lend Me an Ear" resembles for its protagonist Harry Caul's similar collapse into moral solipsism, Duddy tells Crockett and Tubbs, "Everybody wants to know what everybody else is doing, but nobody wants to be the other guy." The trope of watching and being watched is put to dramatic use as Duddy explains the paranoia that comes with being a surveillance expert and anticipating when he himself will be the subject. "I know a million ways to watch somebody, to listen to somebody, to peel open his secret lives," he tells the detectives, "and now I'm always wondering when *I'll* be the target and how they're going to get *me*."

Ironic on its face, "Lend Me an Ear" exposes the atmosphere of fear and suspicion in which Duddy lives and which is epitomized by his maxim "Always leave yourself a way out." In a fitting coda, Switek suggests to the squad that they give Duddy a taste of his own medicine. The final scene opens on Duddy at his workstation, where the squad has managed to leave him a videotaped message. Four identical images of Crockett appear on a bank of monitors, telling the startled sweeper: "Steve, you know what you did. You'll have to live with that. But just remember, I'll be watching." In this revelatory moment, Duddy realizes he is caught in the web of forces from which he cannot

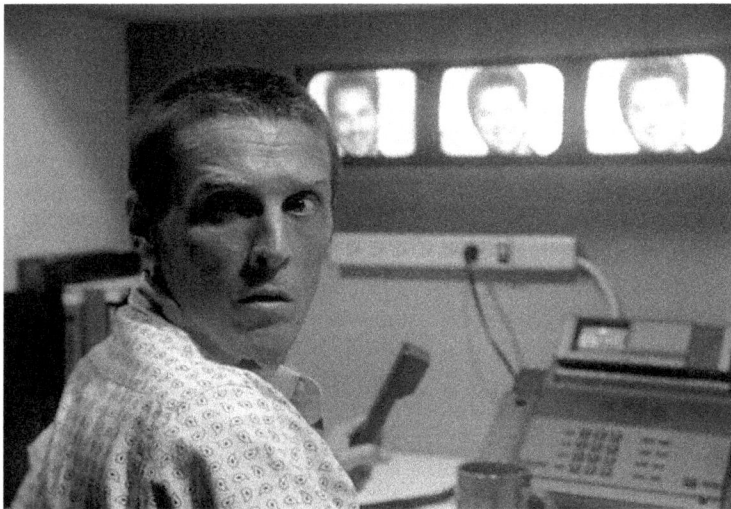

Crockett: "Steve, you know what you did. . . . But just remember, I'll be watching."

free himself and has become what he fears most, the subject of surveillance.

The episodes discussed in this chapter reflect *Miami Vice's* dark mood and ironic tone. The use of the freeze-frame ending in "No Exit" signifies the seriousness with which the gunfire is to be taken; in "Heart of Darkness" it registers a note of finality. In "Heart of Darkness" Arthur Lawson's psychological disintegration is prompted by both his unmooring from moral constraints and his sense of guilt over betrayed loyalties and responsibilities. In "Shadow in the Dark," the Shadow constitutes a projection of Crockett's fears of a divided self that he must struggle to keep in check. The philosophical perplexities about knowledge that give "Lend Me an Ear" so much of its thematic heft can be seen in the predicament of Steve Duddy, whose worst fears are confirmed when he runs out the thread of his own opportunism.

Despite the emphasis in these episodes on the existential hazards of undercover police work, *Miami Vice* does not overlook its sheer physical threats. Episodes that place the principal characters in jeopardy include those in which Lou Rodriguez is struck and killed by a bullet meant for Crockett ("Calderone's Return, Part 1: The Hit List"), Larry Zito is murdered ("Down for the Count"), and Gina Calabrese is raped ("To Have and to Hold"). Gina and Trudy are abducted and about to be killed in "Yakuza" and Trudy is drugged in "Missing Hours." Tubbs takes beatings in "The Maze" and "Nobody Lives Forever," and Crockett is hospitalized in critical condition from a gunshot wound in "A Bullet for Crockett."

From here we turn to the themes of identity, authenticity, redemption, and the politics of *Miami Vice.* These are explored in episodes that expose to an unprecedented extent in American crime television the dark side of 1980s political culture.

Authenticity, Redemption, and the Politics of *Miami Vice*

A recurring theme in *Miami Vice* is the alienating character of undercover police work in which vice detectives must constantly be on their guard. A treacherous criminal underclass, with its power, wealth, and surfeit of illicit drugs, is bad enough. The desperation of an ever larger number of homeless and dispossessed people, the failure of Marielito refugees to find homes and jobs, and the constant racial and ethnic tensions (discussed in chapter 1) also go with the territory. Once Crockett and Tubbs infiltrate the criminal underground as drug dealers Sonny Burnett and Rico Cooper, they must confront their fears of being discovered and how their true identities are jeopardized. In chapter 2, we saw this given dramatic expression in the predicament of Arthur Lawson, who felt the need to give himself over to the satisfaction of the transgressive desires he has repressed and at the same time to maintain his role as a respected representative of law and order.

Because Crockett must retain his identity over time as a vice detective even as he masquerades as Burnett, his performance brings into relief the constructed nature of his role. Twenty years after the debut of the series, when Michael Mann spoke about what he called "the core" of the Sonny Crockett character, he recalled a line from Anthony Yerkovich's pilot. Gina Calabrese asks Crockett, "Do you sometimes forget who you are?" and Crockett replies, "Darlin', I sometimes *remember* who I am." The undercover vice detective who must of necessity identify with his role always faces the possibility that he will be consumed by it. Of course, one might contend that Crockett's performances as Burnett by definition call his authenticity into question. Against this it might be argued that for Crockett's actions to even count as "performances," there must be a basis in the behavior of an authentic self on which such performances supervene. Nevertheless, since it is for the purpose of posing as his undercover persona that Crockett has been provided with the Ferrari, the Scarab boat, the sloop *St. Vitus Dance,* the designer wardrobe, and the Rolex watch, *Miami Vice* invariably raises the question of whether without them he has a stable character of his own.

In the series pilot, Sonny's estranged wife, Caroline, tells him, "You get high on the action," and this remark presages the eventual break-up of their marriage. By the fifth episode, their divorce is final. In the course of the series Crockett has affairs and romantic involvements with a femme fatale with a homicidal husband ("Definitely Miami"), a flight attendant who dies from the cocaine she has smuggled into the country ("Yankee Dollar"), and a French Interpol agent who is in reality an assassin for a sinister organization ("French Twist"). In the episode "Nobody Lives Forever," Crockett is so preoccupied by a new romance with an architect named Brenda (Kim Greist) that he fails to cover Tubbs's back when the latter is in jeopardy. As a result, Tubbs is beaten up during a surveillance assignment that Crockett missed because he overslept at Brenda's house. Tubbs shows up at her door, a bloodied, somber reminder to Crockett that his first commitment must be to the job and his partner. After Crockett falls in love in succession with a drug-addicted physician ("Theresa") and the owner of an escort service that fronts for a prostitution ring ("By Hooker By Crook"), he gives

Gina: "Do you ever forget who you are?" Crockett: "Darlin', I sometimes *remember* who I am!"

ironic expression to his choices in women: "First a junkie, now a hooker. I think I've been in the business too long; I'm starting to fall for the players."

These failed romances and dysfunctional relationships clearly serve as reminders that the emotional life of a vice detective is precarious and seldom in balance. In the fourth season, Crockett marries country/pop singer Caitlin Davies (real-life pop singer Sheena Easton), but this relationship, too, is doomed to failure. The vulnerability of their marriage to fate is indicated by just how quickly their romance blossoms in the four-episode arc. When Caitlin asks Sonny whether they can make their marriage work despite their disparate career paths and he answers that they can, "or die trying," he is telegraphing events that will overtake them and bring Caitlin's life to an abrupt and tragic end.

A Noir Redemptive Pattern

Several key episodes of *Miami Vice*, including "Evan," "Lombard," "The Fix," "One Way Ticket," and "Forgive Us Our Debts," exhibit a redemptive pattern that can be found in classic film noir. In what Palmer (forthcoming) calls "the noir redemption film," the troubled past of the protagonist unexpectedly intrudes on the present, condemning him or her to confront it, often with fatal results, as in *The Strange Love of Martha Ivers* (Lewis Milestone, 1946) and *Out of the Past* (Jacques Tourneur, 1947). Sometimes, however, "this pattern is interestingly transformed, with the intrusion of the past offering a chance at redemption, however painful and compromised" (Palmer forthcoming). The classic noir redemptive pattern can be found in the episode "Evan," discussed above, and in the narrative of the central character of the episode "Out Where the Buses Don't Run," while the "transformed" variation can be found in the narrative of Crockett's encounter with his past when he suffers a concussion and "becomes" his alter ego Burnett. In this and the next section I discuss in turn these variations on the noir redemption pattern.

In "Out Where the Buses Don't Run," the full extent of the principal character's incapacity for redemption is exposed only at the end of the episode. In a virtuoso performance, Bruce McGill is ex-vice detective Hank Weldon. Weldon spent three years making a case against Tony Arcaro, a notorious drug dealer who had an indictment against him dismissed on a technicality, disappeared, and was assumed to be dead. Weldon is obsessed with Arcaro (a man he calls "Mr. Founding Father of Cocaine in Miami"), and when he provides some striking circumstantial evidence to the vice detectives that Arcaro is alive and back in the drug dealing business in town, they cannot help but take notice. In this way, the episode engages what Foster Hirsch has identified as a nearly ubiquitous noir theme, the appearance of the past in the present (1999, 296).

Weldon's behavior is unconventional, even bizarre, which makes it difficult for Crockett and Tubbs to take what he tells them about Arcaro's reappearance at face value. For example, he repeatedly mimics movie and television personalities—Boris Karloff, Walter Brennan, Peter Lorre, Groucho Marx, Mr. Scott from *Star Trek*—in verbal sparring with Crockett and Tubbs, who are trying to stick to business and determine whether he is on the level or simply stringing together a series of uncanny coincidences. He flies into a fit of rage when they express doubt that Arcaro is still alive. "I want Arcaro!" he thunders at the startled detectives. Even more ominously, Weldon's former partner, Marty Lang (David Strathairn), tells the detectives that Weldon's obsession with Arcaro necessitated a medical leave that became a medical discharge from the Vice Division and led to his incarceration in a psychiatric treatment center in Ft. Lauderdale. Crockett and Tubbs are torn between dismissing Weldon as deranged and accepting his contention that Arcaro is indeed operating behind the scenes to get rid of his former criminal associates, who have taken over the drug dealing operation he began in 1962. When Arcaro does not turn up at a drug bust at a Stiltsville dock, contrary to Weldon's assurances that he would, Crockett tells the distraught former detective to give up his quixotic quest. Unwilling or unable to accept that his elusive quarry is dead, Weldon trashes his computer (which he has personified and addresses throughout the episode as "Lorraine"), abandons his shabby apartment, and disappears into the night. Then he phones the vice squad to tell them he has found Arcaro and placed him in custody. "Do you want in or not?" he asks the detectives, and hangs up.

The drive to the location Weldon has given them is filmed in a truck shot that follows Crockett's black Ferrari through the dark, deserted streets of Miami Beach. The mournful Dire Straits' song "Brothers in Arms" on the sound track gives the scene a funereal aspect. When they arrive at a desolate, abandoned building, Weldon tells them to come upstairs to a room

69

where Arcaro is supposed to be. "Funny, he's just a tired old man. Guess he's kind of relieved it's over. Spilled it all. He's in here," he tells them. "There's no one here, Hank," Tubbs says as he looks around the small room. "He's right there," Weldon replies, as he picks up a sledgehammer and smashes through the drywall to reveal Arcaro, partially decomposed and wearing his characteristic beige suit and straw hat. Back-up police arrive at the scene accompanied by Marty Lang, who knew Weldon had killed Arcaro and admits he helped him build the wall. Lang now tells the detectives, "He was my partner. You understand? You understand?" Ultimately, Weldon is lost in a noir void, neither redeemed nor justified.

Redemption and Existential Choice

A four-episode narrative arc that begins with the last episode of the fourth season and continues into the fifth season dramatizes the subjective experience of Crockett's commitment to raise himself from the depraved state into which he has fallen in the persona of Sonny Burnett. These episodes illustrate the second type of noir redemptive strategy described by Palmer above, depicting how Crockett handles the problem of a self in crisis as he seeks to restore agency to that part of him he has surrendered to his criminal alter ego.

The moral universe of *Miami Vice* shifts radically in "Mirror Image," the last episode of season four. Crockett's unassimilated grief over the death of his wife Caitlin and his disposition to suppress it lead him to undertake an ill-starred undercover mission during which he sustains a severe head injury. As a result, Crockett begins to suffer from amnesia and display symptoms of dissociative personality disorder, coming to believe that he is Sonny Burnett. He moves from Miami to Ft. Lauderdale, where he goes to work for Miguel Manolo (Tony Atzio), a Colombian crime boss. Crockett's transformation into Burnett is so convincing that in short order he becomes a trusted member of the Manolo organization and a busy participant in its criminal enterprises. Undercover, Crockett's vices—his tendency to cynicism, his excessive zeal—become Burnett's virtues. On a symbolic level, the white linen jackets and pastel silks give way to dark colors and coarser fabrics as Crockett descends into the criminal underworld believing he is Burnett.

Traumatized and transformed, Crockett appears on the scene in season five bearing significant psychological wounds because he has been deprived of the memories out of which his identity as Crockett is formed. But then, as his memories seep back into his consciousness, he begins to revisit the narrative of his own past, indicated by a series of intermittent flashbacks. Although as Crockett, he is driven by his need to reclaim his identity, he is thwarted by Burnett's nihilism, as evidenced by the criminal acts he commits on behalf of Manolo. As Burnett, he pays a price far higher than suffering the anxieties of nightmares and recurring flashbacks to his former identity as Crockett. He undergoes an inexorable decline into feelings of helplessness, hopelessness, and guilt. Increasingly tormented by flashbacks—a joke with Tubbs, a tender moment with Caitlin—that he cannot reconcile with the life he is living as Burnett, he manages to trace back his history to the Vice Division, where he shows up to confront his past.

A redemptive leap of faith into the saving embrace of religion is out of the question in the resolutely secular world of *Miami Vice,* so Crockett's redemption must be fashioned from the materials of his own existential freedom. As the themes of restoring his true identity and living authentically are worked out in the episode "Redemption in Blood," Crockett puts himself in a life-threatening situation that pits him against a wily and ruthless adversary, Cliff King (played by Matt Frewer, TV's "Max Headroom"). King has taken over the drug operation that Crockett-as-Burnett once controlled. Crockett knows that King has entered into an alliance with a renegade Mexican military officer (Victor Argo) to import drugs into the United States,

Crockett traces his past back to the Vice Division to confront the killer inside him.

so he resolves to regain control of the operation and entrap King by masquerading as Burnett. The choice Crockett makes to enter into such an extreme situation is, for the existential protagonist, the resolution of his crisis. In summoning up the motivational energy to take action against an uncertain and life-threatening backdrop (Rybin 2007, 118), Crockett confronts the anxiety of the dangerous situation and in the process affirms his authenticity. Out of the existential expression of his freedom he emerges as his authentic self and reclaims his identity. *Miami Vice* thus dramatizes the idea that authenticity is achieved through highly individualized styles of thought and action, in which existential choice is the ultimate redemptive act. Further, while still rejecting the most extreme implications of film noir's fatalism, the series suggests that the past plays a significant role in forming the protagonist's character and conflicts.[1]

In "Bad Timing," the final episode of the arc, Crockett submits to psychological counseling and voices aloud the question that has been eating at him. "What kind of a person *am* I?" Crockett asks, giving expression to the confusion and despair of the noir protagonist who seeks to avoid the loss of his identity (Hirsch 1999, 227). In his first session with the police therapist, Crockett talks about the stresses and confusions of undercover work in which he is alienated because he is always playing a role as someone else. As Crockett confronts the alienation that follows from his need to enact a series of masquerades over the course of his career on the vice squad, he achieves a moment of existential recognition that reaffirms his identity and, not coincidentally, facilitates the restoration of narrative continuity required for completion of the series. This theme might also seem self-reflexive in that a similar situation could apply to Don Johnson himself. After all, it is Johnson who must masquerade as Crockett in order to ground the problem Crockett has in having to masquerade as Burnett. *Miami Vice* is thus self-reflexive in the sense that it is a vehicle that promotes its lead actor as much as it is a drama about its main character.

New Forms of Noir and the Politics of *Miami Vice*

So far I have discussed the politics of *Miami Vice* only in passing in order to fully explain the show's noir aesthetic and the themes it helped to develop. In addition to serving up intense dramas of the lives of undercover police detectives, the show followed out an agenda of political critique and commentary and explored, in Richard Martin's words, "the enduring sociopolitical legacy of the Reagan-Bush administrations on American society" (1997, 121–22). Unlike classic film noir, which founded the breakdown of the American dream in social inequality and economic deprivation, *Miami Vice* locates the dissolution of the American dream in the corruption of U.S. foreign policy—specifically in its aim to achieve hemispheric if not global hegemony. According to Christopher Sharrett, "The lonely plight of Sonny Crockett and Rico Tubbs . . . conveyed the moody, fatalistic, defeated outlook that was perhaps the truest reflection of the Reagan era" (2000, 42). The ubiquity of this theme in Michael Mann's feature films leads Steven Rybin to connect them with Mann's generally progressive political outlook—one inflected by "Mann's melancholy regarding the possibilities of human agency in the desolate landscapes of late capitalism" (2007, 114). Throughout its five seasons *Miami Vice* dramatized this theme with an increasingly heavy hand while leaving room for Crockett and Tubbs to retain their own integrity at the series end.

Miami Vice reinvented film noir for television in a context that fit the sociopolitical realities of mid-1980s America with its post–Vietnam War doubts and lack of national purpose, its inner city pathologies and violence, and its Reagan-era political scandals. With the collapse of the Soviet Union and the rise of powerful and elusive terrorist organizations, 1980s television gave expression to new forms of noir. Transformations in the conception of the noir protagonist and the dark forces he or she had to face can be found in the series finale of *Miami Vice*, in the second season of *Crime Story*, and in *The X-Files* and *24*, shows in which U.S. dominance is the motivating force for the criminal acts of conspirators or individuals in the employ of government (often the two are indistinguishable). Michael Moses argues that in place of the femme fatale and communism, the new noir increasingly sees government itself, and particularly the government of the United States, as the source of the darkness and disorder that endanger the world (2008, 222). The world thus disclosed is one of criminal violence, governmental power, and political corruption that reflect the dark side of the human condition and an American society whose moral center cannot hold. This is not to say that *Miami Vice* endorsed a thoroughgoing nihilism. The political critique to be found in the episodes discussed below implies a commitment to values that are not up for grabs or merely chosen, values that are shown through the way Crockett, Tubbs, and Castillo respond to the corruption they encounter and their powerlessness to prevent it.

This critique, expressed in the form of sowing seeds of mistrust in the foreign policy objectives and methods of the U.S. government, is introduced early in the first season in "No Exit," an episode discussed in chapter 2 and one worth revisiting in view of its relevance to the present topic. Federal agents join Crockett and Tubbs in their surveillance of the arms dealer Tony Amato in order to catch him in the act of selling the Stinger missiles his men have stolen from a National Guard armory. The FBI wants to bust Amato as soon as they learn he is in possession of the Stingers, but Crockett and Tubbs protest vehemently. In their view, they can have it all: Amato, the Stingers, and the original buyer—a Jamaican they are holding in custody—if the deal goes down as planned, with Tubbs posing as the buyer. The bust proceeds and Amato is taken into custody. But when he is brought to his arraignment, he is intercepted on the steps of the Dade County courthouse by representatives of an unnamed federal agency who demand his release because Amato is a conduit who can supply arms to certain factions in Central and South America without causing embarrassment to the United States. "I got the *juice*," Amato boasts as Castillo is compelled to remove the handcuffs from his prisoner. (As previously noted, this is by no means the end of Amato's troubles.)

The episode "Baseballs of Death" proceeds in a similar vein. Brody (Mark Metcalf), a renegade DEA agent, is the conduit between an arms dealer, Speed Stiles (Oliver Platt), and a Chilean police chief, Ernesto Guerrero (Tony Plana), who is in Miami to buy anti-personnel canisters, the so-called "baseballs of death" that give the episode its title. This comes to the attention of Crockett and Tubbs because Guerrero is the leading suspect in the murder of a prostitute and her pimp. Brody intervenes when the vice detectives attempt to arrest Guerrero, explaining to them that the agency often helps Guerrero obtain arms on the black market because "he helps us take out the garbage" in places where an overt U.S. presence might cause trouble.

By far the most explicit treatment of the issue comes in the episode most conspicuously informed by a narrative of political and corporate corruption, the two-hour second season opener, "The Prodigal Son." Crockett and Tubbs come to New York as Burnett and Cooper to investigate the activities of a South American drug cartel whose operations have led to the deaths of DEA agents in Bogota, Miami, and points north. They learn that both local law enforcement and multinational corporations are complicit in these crimes. In particular, the episode represents New York City bankers as the silent partners of the Revilla brothers' Colombian drug cartel, a depiction that reaches a dramatic climax in a confrontation between Crockett and Tubbs and J. J. Johnston (Julian Beck), the banking executive who has ordered a hit on the pair. He tells them in no uncertain terms that there is no way he and his colleagues in the financial community are going to let the South American countries they have propped up default on their loans, even if that means turning a blind eye to their largest cash crop, cocaine. This leads Crockett to tell him: "I can't touch you. I know that. Too many roadblocks, politics, favors. But you're dirty, Ace. And I'm patient."

In previous chapters I pointed out ways *Miami Vice* defied the conventions of the police detective genre. The three episodes I have just described call attention to a fourth. While Greater Miami is *Miami Vice*'s locus and center of narrative gravity, the criminal activities to which the investigations of Crockett and Tubbs are directed extend to Cuba ("Heroes of the Revolution"), Chile ("Baseballs of Death"), Nicaragua ("Stone's War"), Vietnam ("The Savage"), and Thailand ("Golden Triangle") in a global network of arms and drug trafficking and political corruption.

The episodes of *Miami Vice* that expose its politics are usually influenced by U.S. foreign policy and how it impinges upon

Crockett to New York City banker J. J. Johnston (Julian Beck): "I can't touch you. I know that. But you're dirty, Ace. And I'm patient."

actual events. Increasingly during seasons two and three, Reagan administration policies inspire episodes that offer critiques of the United States' pursuit of empire. For example, "Stone's War," "The Savage," and "Baseballs of Death" purport to expose the use of U.S. mercenaries in Nicaragua, the willingness of the CIA to employ an operative who assassinates left-of-center and communist political leaders and diplomats around the world, and the propensity of the DEA to circumvent the embargo on arms to Chile, respectively. This critique is subsequently staged on a very broad front, as in the series finale, "Freefall," which indicts the entire apparatus of federal law enforcement for its complicity with a corrupt foreign policy.

In "Golden Triangle, Part 2," an episode co-written by Michael Mann, Castillo's arch-nemesis, Lao Li, a powerful Chinese drug lord, comes to live in Miami, courtesy of the CIA.

Castillo demands that the agency's liaison with Lao Li, ex-CIA agent Dale Menton (John Santucci), tell him where he has Lao Li stashed. Menton sarcastically dismisses the suggestion that Lao Li is in hiding or that he has any intention other than to live in Miami as an honored citizen: "Castillo, nobody's hiding from you. Nobody's running away from you. Because as far as everyone's concerned, you're not a threat anymore. You're nothing anymore."

During Castillo's tenure in the DEA, his unit planned a raid on Lao Li's men who were smuggling opium out of central Asia for sale in the United States. The unit was ambushed and most of Castillo's men were killed. Castillo now asks Menton who ratted out his unit. In a colloquy worth quoting at length, Menton tells Castillo his problem in Southeast Asia was that he never knew when to back off: "You DEA bozos want to interdict

Ex-CIA operative Dale Menton (John Santucci) to Castillo: "You're not a threat anymore. You're nothing anymore."

opium at the source, fine, interdict anybody's opium you want. But we told you, do not interdict Lao Li's opium, 'cause his junk was financed by politicians in Bangkok, 'cause we needed to keep them clowns happy. But no, not you, you're by the book on the straight and narrow and willing to compromise our interests just to knock over a little bit of number 3."

Castillo is contemptuous: "*A little bit of number 3.* There were two-and-a-half tons coming out of the Shan Mountains to be refined into heroin of number 3 opium. The men your agency sponsored were responsible for hundreds of lives . . ."

Menton is unapologetic:

> Don't start singin' that song to me 'cause I don't give a damn how many junkies end up dying in Detroit with a needle stickin' in their arm. If they didn't score Lao Li's they'd score Turkish smack, Mexican brown, one kind of smack or another kind of smack, what the hell difference does it make? What *does* make a difference is that the opium your people busted caused political problems for us in Thailand, and in case you ain't boned up on recent history lately, that happens to be the last piece of real estate we've got access to in that part of the world. You want to know who ratted you out? *I did,* I ratted you out, you arrogant bastard. I set up the ambush of the caravan, I gave them your position, your strength, and they hit you from the *back*!

In his role as Martin Castillo, Edward James Olmos's minimalist characterization of the brooding lieutenant provides the gravitas that effectively contrasts with Crockett's relentless sarcasm and Tubbs's buttoned-up cool. Castillo's reticence masks the contained emotion of a man who is kept in check by enormous reserves of integrity and discipline, but even these have their limits, and after he hears Menton's disclosure, Castillo grasps him by the throat with one hand (keeping his other arm firmly in his pocket) and forces him down onto the conference room table. Crockett and Tubbs have to intervene to get him to loosen his grip.

The mood of the two episodes "Back in the World" and "Stone's War," from seasons two and three, respectively, with their characterizations of Ira Stone (Bob Balaban) that gradually disclose his complex psychology, becomes increasingly ominous. Influenced by actual developments in U.S. foreign policy, these episodes combine political disillusion with pessimism and despair. Here freedom and power are two sides of the same coin, and as so often happens in *Miami Vice,* the loss of the chance at redemption is tied to the protagonist's existential impasse. These episodes explore Stone's efforts to attain or regain authenticity in the face of hopelessness and the fear of irreversible loss of power. *Miami Vice* invests these narratives with the theme of complicity between government, media, and criminal enterprises and the need of the first to co-opt law enforcement at the local level to facilitate the smooth execution of large-scale government policies.

The opening flashback sequence of "Back in the World" begins with documentary footage of the evacuation of Saigon in April 1975 as the victorious North Vietnamese are about to enter the city. Songs by The Doors consolidate the episode's early seventies ambience. U.S. helicopters take refugees on board and aircraft carriers steam away. We cut to the interior of one of the ships where war correspondent Stone has taken a reluctant infantryman, Sonny Crockett, into the hull of the ship to witness what he has discovered. Body bags with soldiers killed in action are also carrying bags of heroin that, Stone insists, are the private stash of a mysterious supply sergeant known in country as "Captain Real Estate." "Isn't it ironic, man?" Stone keeps asking. When we return to the present, Crockett and Tubbs have just witnessed an abortive DEA drug bust at a remote airstrip that has netted a mere two pounds of marijuana. As they are about to take their leave, a helicopter carrying Ira Stone lands, and the two stare at each other for a moment and then embrace.

Stone, the former war correspondent, wants Crockett's help in tracking down Colonel William Maynard, who, Stone tells Crockett, can help him locate the drug smuggling sergeant. Crockett does not yet realize that Maynard is the smuggler, Captain Real Estate. Nor does he know that Stone himself has been in and out of detox numerous times for a drug habit and is preparing to blackmail Maynard, the renegade officer turned drug dealer. In an inspired job of casting, Maynard is played by G. Gordon Liddy, an operative of the White House "Plumbers" unit that carried out the notorious break-in of the Democratic National Committee headquarters at the Watergate Hotel complex in 1972, for which he served four and a half years in prison. Liddy is regarded by some as the model for Maynard, given his reputation as a loose cannon in his willingness to serve the Nixon administration by engaging in various illegal activities (which did not, however, include drug dealing or murder, as in the case of Maynard).

A confrontation between Maynard and Stone occurs at Maynard's home, with Crockett in attendance as a confused onlooker. Stone issues a vituperative denunciation of Maynard and the policies he implemented as a functionary for the Pentagon: "The world is a world of hurt because you and guys like you are always spookin' around in it with your duplicitous games and your assassins and your extreme prejudice." After Stone drives away in Crockett's car, leaving the vice detective stranded, Maynard tells Crockett, "Maybe the war covered Stone, Sonny. You ever think about that?"

"Back in the World" recalls Carol Reed's 1949 noir classic *The Third Man*. Like the shadowy figure Harry Lime (Orson Welles) who sells diluted penicillin to hospitals in postwar Vienna, causing widespread misery and death, Maynard is trying to unload the rapidly decomposing heroin he smuggled into the United States. His buyers include Vietnam War veterans in Miami who are dying from the drugs tainted by wood alcohol used to preserve the corpses in which the heroin was hidden on its way back from Vietnam. In his investigation of these deaths, Crockett is forced to recognize the inescapability of his Vietnam War past through the person of Ira Stone; this *Out of the Past* motif is an excellent example of how *Miami Vice* manufactures a noir narrative out of post–Vietnam War trauma.

"Stone's War" is even more oppressive than "Back in the World." On a narrative and visual level, the episode depicts Contra-type soldiers killing peasants and a priest in a rural village in Nicaragua. Stone obtains videotaped evidence of the paramilitary unit, ostensibly recruited by Maynard in the United States to carry out the illegal combat mission. The bleak, uncompromising ending of "Stone's War," in which Stone is killed, Maynard escapes, and the cause of the civilian deaths is covered up by the U.S. government and a complicit media, reflects perhaps a sense of resignation about the Iran-Contra scandal and a political object lesson about Reagan administration policy in Nicaragua. And in a striking confluence of the fictional and the real, a week after the broadcast of "Stone's War," an American plane carrying supplies to the Contras was shot down over Nicaragua (O'Connor 1986b, 31).

The politics of *Miami Vice* thus encompass not only the characterization of metropolitan Miami as a violent city with its drug trafficking, arms dealing, and gang warfare. It also implies its foreign and alienating character and reaffirms U.S. military adventures and revelations of intrigue and malfeasance at the highest levels of government. These in turn reflect less a matter of the failure of law enforcement to stop the flow of illegal drugs into the United States and more a matter of being unable to alter the political ideology that makes it possible.

In the series finale, "Freefall," Crockett and Tubbs recognize the limits of their ability to alter political events that have disclosed the corrupt policies and practices to which they cannot reconcile themselves. In "Freefall" we witness a new attitude toward concentrated state power, as the episode confirms the conspiracy between the U.S. government, a Latin American dictator, and the drug cartels. The message seems clear: an imperial, militaristic, corporatist America is determined to entrench its empire. "There's only two things that count," the high official of an unnamed U.S. federal agency tells Crockett and Tubbs at the episode's end, when their attempts to bring the dictator to justice have failed. "American interests and anything that's counter to 'em." Thus conspiracy and hegemony are identified as the real engines of U.S. foreign policy. As Crockett and Tubbs grasp the scope of the government's complicity, they begin to understand the dimensions of a corruption they cannot combat. In a gesture of defiance that recalls Gary Cooper's sheriff in *High Noon* (Fred Zinnemann, 1952), a film often interpreted as a metaphor for the failure of Americans to stand up to Senator Joe McCarthy's anticommunism crusade, Crockett and Tubbs toss their badges to the ground and walk away.

Crockett: "Ever consider a career in southern law enforcement?" Tubbs: "Maybe . . . May*be*."

In the end, Crockett and Tubbs do not succumb to the lure of vice. But are they too demoralized to function in law enforcement at all? In a striking display of narrative closure, *Miami Vice* turns back on itself with the same dialogue between the pair that ended the series pilot. Crockett asks: "Ever consider a career in southern law enforcement?" Tubbs replies: "Maybe . . . may*be*." This final dialogue is a dramatic expression of their lives that reinforces their fates-in-the-making as they leave behind five years as partners in the Vice Division, driving south toward an unknown future.

Why *Miami Vice* Matters

It is now time to explain how *Miami Vice* achieved the emblem of cultural meaning it so conspicuously bears. Of course, by this point in the book it should be obvious why people cared, and continue to care, about *Miami Vice,* so my explanation is likely to seem redundant. Nevertheless, some threads can be pulled together along with assorted controversies and criticisms so that we may remove any lingering doubts about whether, and why, *Miami Vice* matters.

"Why does *Miami Vice* matter?" is at once historical, sociological, aesthetic, and philosophical. The historical context and social conditions of the production and consumption of a prime-time television program provide the basis of an explanation of its status. From an aesthetic and philosophical perspective, the visual, aural, and thematic characteristics are essential to understanding *Miami Vice*'s audience appeal, influence, and cultural importance. No doubt all these factors play a part in our understanding of the show's significance, in its own time and in ours. In the preceding chapters, I have approached the program aesthetically, thematically, and philosophically without turning a blind eye to those features of the historical and social milieu that influenced its production and reception. For example, with its emphasis on the various subcultures in which the professionals of the Vice Division operated, *Miami Vice* used its South Florida locations as a metaphor for both political and cultural conflict. Here, however, I want to address some of the misunderstandings and criticisms of those who deny that *Miami Vice* deserves the milestone status for which I have argued in this book.

Postmodern Noir for the Small Screen

Though the output of noir feature films diminished in the late fifties and sixties, network television in both the United States and the United Kingdom bears the legacy of film noir with *Peter Gunn, Johnny Staccato, The Fugitive, Danger Man* (aka *Secret Agent*), and *The Prisoner. Miami Vice* perpetuated the noir tradition by employing classic noir protagonists and themes (crime, entrapment, alienation, moral ambivalence, corruption). Enriching these themes, *Miami Vice* added such stylistic devices as tight close-ups, music-driven narratives, hand-held sequences, slow motion, and freeze-frame endings. Jan Hammer's score and Jeffrey Howard's art deco color palette suggested how the noir world supervened on the most innocent-appearing details of everyday life, even in sunny South Florida. For such reasons I have referred to "sunshine noir" to denote not only the style of the series but also the style of Miami itself.

Miami Vice fused art-house cinema and popular culture for the small screen at a time when so-called neo-noir feature films were entering a second wave in the 1980s following the achievements of *Chinatown* (Roman Polanski, 1974) and *The Conversation.* The capacity of *Miami Vice* to give its characters and themes a noir inflection and infiltrate prime time gave television audiences a new experience, significantly different from the Cold War narratives of 1950s and 1960s television crime drama. With the thematizing of alienation, moral ambiguity, and the fragmentation of personal identity, and its skeptical attitude toward technology and American capitalist society, the show embraced a politically progressive critique and commentary that reflected post-Vietnam doubts about America's national purpose and moral stature. As we saw in chapter 3, these doubts were shaped by the way *Miami Vice* contrasted the ideals of law enforcement with what it conveyed as the realities of political and corporate corruption.

Miami Vice transformed the television cop subgenre and defied its conventions along several lines. For one thing, unlike most police detectives in prime-time television up to that time, Crockett and Tubbs worked as a team that was like a family, with all the ties of loyalty that the latter inspires. For another, unlike earlier site-specific programs, the criminal activities with which the Vice Division was concerned were not confined to the Miami metropolis but extended to other countries, because the market for drug trafficking, gun running, and prostitution is international. The undercover formula of *Miami Vice* accommodated numerous character types that went beyond the usual stereotypes, including the arms merchant ("No Exit"), the drug smuggler ("The Prodigal Son," "Yankee Dollar," "The Great McCarthy"), the combat journalist ("Back in the World," "Stone's War"), the surveillance expert ("Lend Me an Ear"), the terrorist ("When Irish Eyes Are Crying," "French Twist"), and the criminal psychopath ("Shadow in the Dark," "The Savage," and "The Cell Within"). There is even a cocaine-peddling philosophy professor who tells Gina and Trudy, working undercover as college students, "Hey, pump some of this in you, you'll know the true meaning of *Being and Nothingness!*"

Of course, not every episode of the show worked. Some were poorly conceived, badly written, or photographed without distinction. According to the responses on the websites *TV.com* and *Miami Vice* Chronicles, fans took a dim view of "Missing Hours," though one may wonder whether the episode's oneiric aspect was underappreciated or went unnoticed. Other episodes do not work as suspense or melodrama. And some seem

87

half-baked. *Miami Vice* had its share of contrived or implausible plots that were unredeemed even by the characteristic banter between Crockett and Tubbs, and it is fair to say that bad episodes were especially disappointing because the show usually met its own high standards.

Much of Michael Mann's feature film work concerns the problematic nature of living authentically, a thread that gives *Miami Vice* its existential edge. The thematic parallels of "Shadow in the Dark" to Mann's own *Manhunter* (1986) are undeniable. Looked at from this perspective, *Miami Vice* is a series about not only the particular assignments of the detectives in the Vice Division, but also undercover police work in its riskiest and most terrifying entirety. The show managed to engage with the patterns of contingency in which undercover work is inevitably enmeshed, an indication of what Andrew Spicer calls "a continuing exploration of the underside of the American Dream" (2002, 149). By tracing the steps Crockett and Tubbs must take to infiltrate drug trafficking operations, arms dealing enterprises, and an assortment of scams involving gambling, blackmail, and prostitution, the show adds drama to the inherently ambiguous situation they face when they try to internalize their fabricated identities and somehow recover their authentic selves once the assignment is over. *Miami Vice* shows the risk of being trapped inside a role as well as the psychological cost that comes with the need to perpetually suppress and recover one's true identity. The moments of searing self-disclosure between Crockett and Tubbs, as in "Evan," or between Crockett and Castillo in "Child's Play," which shows Crockett's agony over shooting a child while on duty, develop aspects of character that were rare for crime television in the mid-1980s even if they are commonplace now. The depth of these stories led viewers to care about the principal characters and to want to know more.

In terms of production values and audience appeal, *Miami Vice* occupies a unique niche in 1980s crime television. Not only does it embody the legacy of film noir in such exemplary episodes as "Heart of Darkness," "Definitely Miami," "Death and the Lady," "Streetwise," and "Payback," but its various episodes also incorporate elements of political intrigue and the espionage genre ("French Twist," "Free Verse," "Cuba Libre"), comedy ("Made for Each Other," "Phil the Shill," "The Big Thaw," "The Cows of October"), the psychological thriller ("Out Where the Buses Don't Run," "Little Miss Dangerous," "Shadow in the Dark"), science fiction ("Missing Hours"), and melodrama ("Sons and Lovers," "By Hooker by Crook," "God's Work," "Like a Hurricane").

Many episodes illustrate how both advanced televisual techniques and superlative writing accelerated the transformation of the crime television series from the single-genre police procedural or crime melodrama to the mixed-genre, multiple storyline, thematically adventuresome episodes that draw attention to their own narrative construction, as with a number of 1980s and 1990s neo-noir films such as *Reservoir Dogs* (Quentin Tarantino, 1992), *Romeo Is Bleeding* (Peter Medak, 1994), and *Pulp Fiction* (Quentin Tarantino, 1994). While this does not show that *Miami Vice* directly influenced these films, it is noteworthy that *Miami Vice* was among the first television crime dramas to import postmodern themes and styles into its narratives.

This approach had its risks in the inherently conservative world of network television, as "Tale of the Goat" illustrates. The episode features Haitian voodoo iconography, shadows, slow motion, honeycomb filters, and scenes shot from low angles to visually convey a noir world of sexual innuendo, violence, and depravity, and to depict the psychotic impulses of its antagonist, Maximilien Ildefonce, aka Legba (portrayed by former *Mod Squad* co-star Clarence Williams III). Jan Hammer's ominous score and singles by The Fixx ("Phantom Living"), Nona Hendryx ("Transformation"), and Red Rider ("Can't Turn Back") reinforce the exotic mise-en-scène. Jim Trombetta, who wrote the episode, recalls being told that his script "showed that I didn't write traditional television." In Trombetta's opinion, ex-

89

ecutives at Universal Pictures, the company that produced the show for NBC, "didn't understand *Vice* and were relieved to go back to 'traditional television'" epitomized by *Murder, She Wrote*.[1]

Popular Culture and Intertextuality

The one hundred and eleven episodes of *Miami Vice* are filled with references and allusions to television, movies, celebrities, and the slogans of consumerist culture, usually done for ironic or comic effect, as when Izzy Moreno quotes tidbits of Lee Iacocca's business philosophy in support of one of his cockeyed schemes. The names of characters like Evan Freed, Charlie Glide, Bobby Profile, Milton Glantz, and Steve Duddy subvert the putative realism of the episodes in which they appear, re-

90

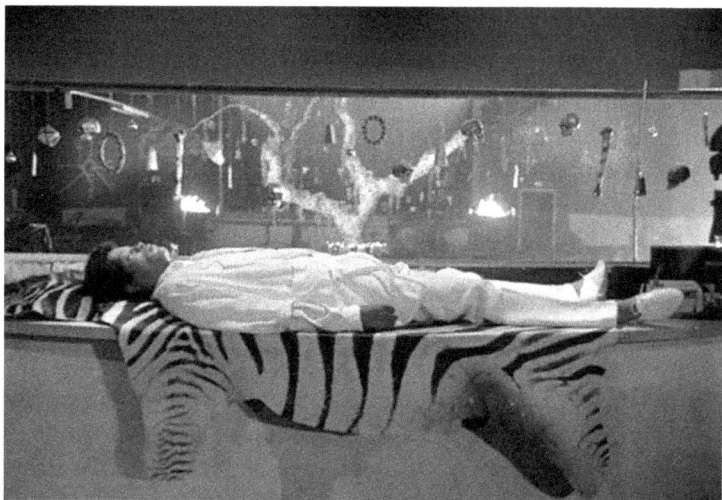

Non-traditional television: "Tale of the Goat" conveys a noir world of sexual innuendo, violence, and depravity, as Legba returns to Miami to resume his criminal activities.

minding us of the dark humor of writers such as Charles Willeford and Elmore Leonard.

The show's immersion in popular culture can be seen in references to Elvis Presley, Michael Jackson, Lee Iacocca (who makes an appearance as a park commissioner in "Sons and Lovers"), Hugh Hefner, *Casablanca, 101 Dalmations, Sky King* ("Out of the blue of the Western sky"), *Red River, Dragnet,* UFOs, tabloids, televangelists, game shows, zombies, and NASCAR racing. Celebrity guest stars from popular music include Phil Collins, Frank Zappa, James Brown, Little Richard, Miles Davis, Glenn Frey, Sheena Easton, Power Station, and the Fat Boys.

A number of *Miami Vice* episode titles allude to film and literature ("Heart of Darkness," "No Exit," "Made for Each Other," "Nobody Lives Forever," "Sons and Lovers," "The Big Thaw," "Lend Me an Ear"). References to television include no fewer than four instances in which a character takes aim and puts a bullet into the TV tube (alluding, of course, to the famous episode in which Elvis Presley shot a hole in his TV set, an event satirized in the episode "Phil the Shill"). Crockett alludes to *Hawaii Five-O* in the episode "Sons and Lovers" when he turns a suspect over to Gina and Trudy and says "Book 'em, Danno." The episode "Death and the Lady," with Paul Guilfoyle as an avant-garde filmmaker who has a woman stabbed in one of his films, is, arguably, a thinly veiled reference to novelist and filmmaker Norman Mailer, who actually stabbed his second wife, Adele Morales, with a penknife after a party, and who titled a book of his poems *Deaths for the Ladies (and Other Disasters).*

A significant feature of *Miami Vice*'s storytelling technique is the foregrounding of intertexts, with flashbacks to scenes in the pilot episode, visual allusions to other episodes, and the recurring appearance of various secondary characters. Included among the latter are Tubbs's love interest Valerie Gordon (played by seventies blaxploitation icon Pam Grier, in three episodes), with whom he carries on a conflicted relationship, Al Lombard (Dennis Farina, three episodes), Ira Stone (two episodes), Frank Mosca (Stanley Tucci, three episodes), and Frank Hackman (Guy Boyd, two episodes).

I have already described the intertextual references to films such as *The Third Man, High Noon,* and *The Conversation. Miami Vice*'s most distinctive intertext occurs in the episode "Honor among Thieves?" which recalls Fritz Lang's 1931 film *M.* In it, a child murderer (portrayed by Peter Lorre) is sought by the police, who launch a crackdown that makes it more difficult for criminals in the city to go about their business. He is subsequently caught by the criminals who, in the words of Thomas Leitch, "carry him off to a kangaroo court where he pleads an irresistible compulsion for the crimes he finds as repugnant as do his accusers" (2002, 93). In "Honor among Thieves?" a serial murderer has taken four young girls as his victims, drugging, assaulting, and killing them before injecting their bodies with pure cocaine. He turns out to be Paul Delgado (John Bowman), a drug dealer who has promised Crockett and Tubbs (as Burnett and Cooper) to roll over on a Miami crime lord, Polmo (Ramy Zada), who is unknowingly doing business with the undercover detectives. They are compelled to remain at Polmo's residence while he checks them out. But with the killer at large and the police putting pressure on the big dealers as they search for the source of the cocaine found in the bodies of the victims, Polmo convenes a meeting with the city's drug bosses and organizes his own dragnet to catch the killer. Delgado is eventually caught and brought to Polmo's nightclub, where Polmo and the drug bosses conduct a trial. Because Crockett has passed himself off as a lawyer, Polmo appoints him to represent the deranged killer, and it is only then that Delgado reveals himself to Crockett as the contact he and Tubbs have been seeking. Delgado makes it clear to Crockett that if he fails to provide a successful defense he will expose Crockett as a vice detective and they will both be killed.

Crockett frames his defense in terms of Delgado's irresistible impulse to do the terrible things he does. Don Johnson gives a compelling performance as the "defender of the damned" who tries to facilitate the gangsters' entry into Delgado's state of mind. "Oh, you see the horror and you don't want to go but you *must*. My God, gentlemen, that is hell. Can you imagine, any of you, having to live in that hell?" Before this jury of his peers can reach a verdict, Delgado breaks away and climbs to a scaffolding high above the club's dance floor, from which he leaps to his death, landing on Polmo and killing him as well. In true film noir style, the two inert bodies form an "X" to mark the doomed as the police arrive on the scene. The reworking of noir themes here and in other episodes lends further credence to *Miami Vice* as a series that both transmits the legacy of film noir and devises new forms for it.

In true film noir style, the two bodies at the end of "Honor among Thieves?" form an "X" to mark the doomed.

Miami Vice and Its Critics

The affluence and consumerism of the 1980s are part of the social and cultural framework of *Miami Vice.* The novelists, filmmakers, and critics of the period saw social conflict and political uncertainty amid rampant consumerism and exploding popular culture. Michael Mann's *Thief, Manhunter,* and *Crime Story* were prescient in capturing better than most the underlying cultural dislocations and anomie. This makes it all the more disappointing that some critics and commentators dwell on the alleged style-over-substance aspect of *Miami Vice.* Todd Gitlin writes, "In this wonderland of drugs, sex, and rock 'n' roll, things take place for strictly visual reasons" (1986, 152). The television critic of the *New York Times* went so far as to call it "mindless glitz" (O'Connor 1986a), and the *Washington Post* described it as "candy-coated candy—eye candy wrapped in an ear candy shell" (Shales 2002, C01). To say, as does Michael Wood (2006), that "the episodes often look like music videos, an effect enhanced by guest appearances from Phil Collins, Willie Nelson, Little Richard, Miles Davis and many others," may mislead readers unfamiliar with the series. There are only sequences within episodes, not entire episodes, that resemble music videos, and their function is to advance the storyline. For example, in "Calderone's Return, Part 1: The Hit List," Rico and Trudy must warn Sonny and Caroline, who are returning home from the safe house on Key Biscayne, that the assassin who has Crockett's name on his hit list is still at large. Their race to the Crocketts' home in the Ferrari under Russ Ballard's "In the Night" has a thematic context that advances the storyline. It is therefore more accurate to say, with Michael Sragow (1999), that "the series used its soundtrack . . . either to articulate surrounding chaos or to provide a defiant counterpoint." The music provided an expression of and a commentary on themes and storylines dramatized on the small screen. These could be chaotic and defiant, as Sragow points out, but they were often poignant or serene, as in the episodes "Evan" and "Lombard." Of course, music made an enormous contribution to the popularity of the show. *Miami Vice* is the first television show to have both a No. 1 single (Jan Hammer's "*Miami Vice* Theme") and a No. 1 album (the *Miami Vice* sound track) on the pop charts. It is also the first to have two singles in the Top 5 in the same week: Hammer's "*Miami Vice* Theme" and Glenn Frey's "You Belong to the City" from "The Prodigal Son," the episode that opened the second season (DeKnock 1985, 82).

More important, Michael Mann has said that "style just gets you seven minutes of attention" (Romney 1996, 14), and the writer-director-producer clearly had larger ambitions in becoming the show's executive producer. Without denying that the show's visual style and music innovations changed the look and rhythm of television, its thematic elements emphasize that undercover existence is deeply contaminated by the experience of fear, suspicion, betrayal, and paranoia. *Miami Vice* is not only a constellation of images but also a network of ideas connected to the themes of American cultural life in the 1980s. The plots of some of the best episodes are built from an interrogation of representation itself: "Heart of Darkness," "Evan," "Back in the World," and "Mirror Image" aim at exploring the territory of the protagonist's own past. Sonny Crockett's struggle to surmount his existential crisis and to create meaning out of the resources of his own freedom is one of the pervasive themes of *Miami Vice* and in subsequent noir television, as illustrated by the perseverance of Fox Mulder and dedication of Dana Scully (*The X-Files*), the resolve of Jack Bauer (*24*), and the crusading (and clearly obsessive) anti-crime campaign of Mike Torello (*Crime Story*), to take only three prominent examples. Through the thematizing of threats to personal identity and pessimism about American society, *Miami Vice* distinguished itself from other police detective shows of its time. As A. O. Scott observes, "In the history of cop dramas, *Miami Vice* remains an intriguing anomaly,

95

a sleek postmodernist detour on the genre's march toward ever more emphatic realism" (2004, 9).

Butler argues that "the police work in *Miami Vice* is based on masquerade—bordering on entrapment—rather than well reasoned deduction. When . . . Crockett and Tubbs are forced to actually solve a mystery, they perform quite badly as deductive reasoners" (1985, 294). But *Miami Vice* is not a mystery show or whodunit with puzzles that need to be solved, and Sherlock Holmes–style detective work was never in the mix.[2] In most episodes, the vice detectives already know who the drug smuggler, arms dealer, or counterfeiter is; their task is to infiltrate the illegal operation in order to catch the guilty party with the contraband so they can make an arrest. *Miami Vice* was always more interested in illuminating the personal dimension of undercover police work and the toll it took on law enforcement personnel than it was in how the Vice Division solved its cases—to say nothing of exposing the structures of political power that supported criminal activity, and conversely: in a phrase, the interpenetration of crime and politics. By giving a low profile to the "relentlessly procedural" aspects of crime detection, *Miami Vice* at its best "was not about the techniques of crime fighting so much as it was about its existential challenges" (Scott 2004, 9). Because the show placed an emphasis on developing character and creating atmosphere, it retained its influence even after time and the inevitable changes of fashion gave prominence to realistic-looking, forensic-oriented police procedurals such as the *Law & Order* and *CSI* franchise shows.

Only one full-length study of *Miami Vice* has appeared to date, Jean-Paul Trutnau's *A One Man Show? The Construction and Deconstruction of a Patriarchal Image in the Reagan Era: Reading the Audio-Visual Poetics of Miami Vice*. Notwithstanding Trutnau's attention to many of the show's themes and details, his errors are difficult to overlook and his emphases can be puzzling. He complains that "the series appears to make a conservative . . . contribution in terms of not dealing with taboos, AIDS for example" (2005, 238). In fact, the episode "God's Work" does engage seriously with AIDS, and other episodes deal with "taboo" subjects such as incest ("Junk Love"), prostitution ("Rites of Passage"), pornography ("Death and the Lady"), and rape ("Bought and Paid For" and "Hell Hath No Fury").

While this objection is comparatively insignificant, others broach matters of greater importance. For instance, Trutnau writes, "Experimentation with the freeze frame is used to ridicule, parody, and make absurd the female image, as one episode vividly shows with its surreal and dreamlike quality" (2005, 234). But this objection seems wide of the mark. What could the "surreal and dreamlike quality" of one (unidentified) episode have to do with the portrayal of women in general on *Miami Vice*? Trutnau also writes that "cars, fast boats and shades all add to Crockett being 'tough and cool' while at the same time being in control, and thus in power" (235). Without denying the general tendency of the show to feature Crockett in quasi-heroic terms, Trutnau overlooks crucial counterexamples. In "Nobody Lives Forever," for example, Brenda is astonished that Sonny, who was shot at while speaking to her from a phone booth, was not terrified, as she says she would be. Crockett's reply is illuminating: "Who says I'm not terrified? I just don't dwell on it." Crockett does not try to hide the fact that he has normal vulnerabilities and fears, but he understands that he would be paralyzed and unable to do his job if he dwelled on them.

Perhaps the most important shortcoming of Trutnau's study is its curiously skewed emphasis. He believes that "the high level of violence in *Miami Vice* . . . often appears unnecessary, making the series stand out for its depictions of brutality. The question remains: why use violence in such a fashion?" (2005, 243). He then adds: "The controversy surrounding this designer violence leads to the series' most problematic unresolved contradiction: namely, the fashion of the male heroes. Obviously, they cannot afford designer clothes on a mere cop salary, but the series fails to explain this. It seems as if it is part of their undercover job, but that may be too simple an explanation" (Trutnau 2005, 244). This objection seems to have originated with Gitlin, who writes, "Just for openers, the viewer has to take for granted that two Miami cops (1985 take-home pay: $429 a week) can blithely afford the latest and flashiest in cars and clothes" (1986, 152). On a similar note, James A. Inciardi and Juliet L. Dee write in their article "From the Keystone Cops to *Miami Vice:* Images of Policing in American Popular Culture" that "to find real-life cops able to afford a white Ferrari and silk t-shirts is improbable" (1987, 100).

We have already noted *Miami Vice*'s thematization of fabricated identities in its emphasis on wardrobe, so it is difficult to understand why Gitlin, Trutnau, and Inciardi and Dee are so puzzled by how the vice detectives can afford expensive cars and clothing. It is easy enough to understand—episodes such as "Whatever Works" and "Lend Me an Ear" in any event make it clear—that the detectives' wardrobes and Crockett's cars and boats have been confiscated from drug dealers and are owned by the Miami police department. They are on loan to the vice detectives who use them to support their covers as players in the fast life they must appear to be living. Whether this is an accurate depiction of actual undercover procedure in the Vice Division of the city of Miami is not on point because *Miami Vice* is drama, not a documentary-style exploration of one city's undercover police work.[3]

Miami Vice had its detractors from the start. Some were never party to the initial enthusiasm for the show. Gitlin writes that "the throwaway plot is full of holes, and much of the writing is as banal as anything television has seen since *Barnaby Jones*" (1986, 152). But note the lack of specificity. Gitlin does not support his criticism with examples, as if it were unnecessary to do so. Then there are the commentators whose early enthusiasm for the show burned out in short order. In an interrogation of the place of *Miami Vice* in what he calls the "Eighties noir" canon, Robert Arnett writes that "*Miami Vice* was very successful and different, as Butler [1985] pointed out, from standard fare. In its second season, however, it became as sanitized as any mainstream TV cop show" (2006, 129). But this assessment is difficult to reconcile with such hard-hitting, uncompromising episodes as "Out Where the Buses Don't Run," "Junk Love," "Back in the World," and "Little Miss Dangerous" from the show's second season and "Stone's War," "Kill Shot," "Shadow in the Dark," and "Streetwise" from the third.

Another criticism by Gitlin is that "Crocket, Tubbs & Co. often share the frame but stare past each other. . . . They don't have much to say to each other" (1986, 156). Even as perceptive a critic as John Caldwell writes that "dialogue really did not even matter in many episodes" (1995, 66). Spectators of *Miami Vice* are left, in Gitlin's words, to "surrender to the trashy pleasure of sheer look and sound" (1986, 152). Leaving aside Gitlin's questionable use of "trashy," the main problem with this line of criticism is that once again, without specific examples, we are asked to take the critics' word for it. I hope that in quoting extensively from the show's dialogue, I have given readers a chance to decide for themselves whether such criticisms are well founded.

As *Miami Vice* went into its third season, critics were increasingly dismissive; indeed, only three Golden Globe nominations and one Emmy nomination came out of the final three years. The fourth season, when some of the production values associated with Michael Mann had vanished, marked a decisive turning point, a loss of the direction and focus that had marked the show's early years. The best episodes of the season—"Death and the Lady," "Baseballs of Death," "Honor among Thieves?" and "Mirror Image"—had passionate intensity, but the worst lacked all conviction. By its fifth season the show was further blemished by weak scripts. Some critics said that *Miami Vice* had deteriorated so badly that it had become a parody of itself.

Notwithstanding the diminishing returns of its final season, *Miami Vice* was instrumental in rewriting the narrative of crime television and developing new possibilities for noir. An important consequence of *Miami Vice*'s cinematic model was the development of network and cable broadcast crime series such as *Law & Order: Criminal Intent, The Sopranos,* and *CSI: Miami,* shows that are the televisual equivalent of feature films with worldwide audiences in the millions. Like the best films, *Miami Vice* and the programs it influenced engaged with problems of personal identity, authenticity, power, and policy that are still with us. Its hugely influential visual and sound design were put in the service of narratives about the men and women who fought, and sometimes succumbed to, the temptations of vice. As such programs proved, the conventions of film noir could be constantly renewed, and this, too, is a legacy of *Miami Vice* and one reason why it is remembered twenty-five years after its debut. And in the end this is why *Miami Vice* matters: its distinctive contributions were indispensable to the transformation of the police detective subgenre into an art form in its own right.

Life after *Vice*

The *Miami Vice* Feature Film

101

Written and directed by Michael Mann and released in 2006 in both a theatrical version and an unrated director's cut DVD, *Miami Vice* confounded the expectations of many fans of the television series who believed that Mann would remake the show with its 1980s sensibility intact. However, not only does the film not do that, it also does not reflect the sociopolitical contexts of 2006 in quite the same way that the television show did so for the mid-1980s. The film's main achievement may lie in Mann's creation of the context in which drug-dealing can be seen as the corporatist-structured international enterprise it has become in the twenty-first century.

While Steven Rybin makes a convincing case that the film "*Miami Vice* looks and sounds nothing like its television predecessor" (2007, 196), the film succeeds in preserving key themes from the series, chief of which are the alienating effects of undercover police work and the need for existential choice on the part of the protagonists. Unfortunately, the film stints on Crockett (Colin Farrell) and Tubbs (Jamie Foxx) as individuals, to say nothing of the relationship between them. Mann may have believed that his principal characters' backstories were so well inscribed in our collective memory that recapitulation was unnecessary. Whatever the reason, the result is that the film treats moments of disclosure between them less effectively than the way those moments were dramatized in, for example, the episode "Evan" in the first season of the television series.

Why would Mann revisit territory he had staked out in television more than twenty years earlier? Timothy Shary observes that Mann tends to revisit his own work in a spirit of what Shary calls "Kubrickian perfectionism" (2006, 17). Rybin also sees Mann's work as recapitulating certain themes and tropes: "As Mann's body of work has grown over the course of thirty years, his own oeuvre has begun to provide him in recent years with a grab bag of narrative tropes, psychological types, snippets of dialogue, and even pieces of music which are constantly reshaped into consistently distinctive aesthetic effects and thematic meanings in each subsequent film" (189). It is also plausible to suppose that Mann wanted to make a contemporary film of *Miami Vice* so that he could utilize computerized special effects and high-definition digital cameras to achieve a style that was impossible in 1984. It is enough to witness the bravura moments in *Miami Vice* where HD photography is put in the service of Mann's style to appreciate the appeal this opportunity had for the filmmaker.

In the feature film, Mann and his director of photography, Dion Beebe, create aerial shots and sweeping horizontal pans that display Miami at its bejeweled best. Mann's well-known command of detail and ability to choreograph action sequences with precision and verve are on full view in four sequences: a speedboat race that opens the director's cut of the film, an impulsive powerboat junket to Cuba where Crockett and Isabella (Gong Li), a drug lord's lover, have their first romantic moments, the rescue of Trudy (Naomie Harris) from the trailer of the white supremacists who have abducted her, and the climactic shootout.

Mann brings narratives with psychological edge and an existentialist's awareness of life's contingencies to the film. He is as concerned with the problematic nature of living authentically as he was in *Thief*, *Heat*, and *Collateral*. As in the television series, the film shows the risk of identifying too closely with the role dictated by one's undercover mission. When Crockett begins an affair with Isabella, he finds it increasingly difficult to draw the line between his alter ego and true self. It is as if he is in flight from his authentic self, which leads Tubbs to tell his partner, in the film's best line, "There's undercover and there's *which way is up?*" With Crockett's decision not to give himself over completely to Isabella, the film's narrative achieves closure by showing how he temporarily succumbs to, but ultimately resists, the temptations of vice. As we have seen, this is a major theme of the television series as well.

103

Life after *Vice*

Anthony Yerkovich continued to work in crime drama after creating *Miami Vice*. In 1997 he wrote *Hollywood Confidential*, a direct-to-video film in which Edward James Olmos starred as a former L.A. cop who runs a private detective agency. In 2001, Yerkovich wrote and executive produced *The Big Apple* for CBS, which had a brief run. He also executive produced the *Miami Vice* feature film.

Michael Mann has directed a number of feature films, including *The Last of the Mohicans* (1992), *Heat* (1995), the multi-Oscar nominated *The Insider* (1999), *Ali* (2001), and *Collateral* (2004). His television activity includes a short-lived TV series, *Robbery Homicide Division* (2002–3). His recent contribution to the crime genre is the feature film *Public Enemies* (2009).

Dick Wolf is a prolific writer and producer. His many executive producer credits include *Law & Order* (1990 to date), *Law & Order: Special Victim's Unit* (1999 to date), *Law & Order: Criminal Intent* (2001 to date), and *Dragnet* (2003–4).

Don Johnson went from the East Coast and a white Testarossa to the West Coast and a yellow Plymouth Barracuda as the star of the San Francisco–based cop drama *Nash Bridges* (1996–2001). His film credits after *Miami Vice* include *The Hot Spot* (Dennis Hopper, 1990), *Harley Davidson and the Marlboro Man* (Simon Wincer, 1991), *Guilty as Sin* (Sidney Lumet, 1993), and *Tin Cup* (Ron Shelton, 1996).

Philip Michael Thomas appeared in numerous European television productions in the 1990s, as the character Cedric Hawks in episodes of *Nash Bridges* in 1997 and 2001, and as the voice of Lance Vance in *Grand Theft Auto: Vice City* (Navid Khosari, 2002).

Edward James Olmos appeared in many feature films and television productions, including *American Me* (Edward James Olmos, 1992), *Menendez: A Killing in Beverly Hills* (TV, 1994), and *Selena* (Gregory Nava, 1997). In 1995 he was nominated for an Emmy for Outstanding Supporting Actor in a Miniseries or a Special for his work in *The Burning Season*. In 2004 he took a starring role as Admiral William Adama in *Battlestar Galactica* (2004–8).

Jan Hammer has an active career as a composer and performer. In the 1990s he began a busy agenda scoring for films and television. In addition to releasing new (non-*Vice*) albums and re-releasing a number of albums from his early career, he has released albums of *Vice* music, including *Miami Vice: The Complete Collection* (2002) and *The Best of Miami Vice* (2004).

Introduction

1. I discuss the nature, history, philosophical dimensions, and exemplary instances of noir television in "An Introduction to the Philosophy of TV Noir" in Sanders and Skoble 2008, 1–29.
2. David Chase interview accessed at http://www.pbs.org/newshour/bb/entertainment/july-dec01/chase_8–8.html
3. Interviews and profiles of Mann provided indispensable background for this study. See Sanders and Palmer 2010.
4. The interview with Dick Wolf can be found in the *Archive of American Television* series, part 3 of 7, March 25, 2003.

Chapter 1

1. A useful survey of pre-eighties noir style on television can be found in Ursini 1996.
2. Michael Mann told Art Harris (1985), "We changed the image of Miami. We took its cultural essence, falsified what it looked like with selective art direction and put it on TV. Now Miami is trying to make itself look like the Miami on the show. It's trying to conform reality to our fiction."
3. Martin does not use the term "sunshine noir" and he is not talking about *Miami Vice* here but about the world conveyed by nineties' film noir. It argues for my thesis regarding the legacy of film noir that his description applies to *Miami Vice* so well. J. Hoberman (2007) contends that "sunshine noir" is a particular subset of film noir that deals

with local history, particularly Hollywood's.

4. Smith reports the figure as being "about $50,000 a week to buy the rights to three or four contemporary musical selections as they were originally recorded" (1985, C20).

5. Hirsch (1999, 259) makes a similar point about the moral conservatism of the neo-noir heist film *Reservoir Dogs*.

Chapter 2

1. Key existentialist documents include Jean-Paul Sartre, *Being and Nothingness* (1943, published in English in 1956) and "Existentialism Is a Humanism" (1945), and Albert Camus, *The Stranger* (1942) and *The Myth of Sisyphus* (1943). Robert Porfirio (1976) provides a seminal study of existentialist themes in film noir.

2. O.N.C. Wang (1988) finds fault with this episode because it "safely defuses the issue by turning it into a drama of male heterosexual bonding" (11).

3. The image of the writer whose books "give us reality as it really is, through a pane of glass," goes back to Zola, as James Wood (2005) points out in his discussion of literary realism and its postmodern critics.

Chapter 3

1. For discussion of the inherent conflict between existentialism and film noir's fatalism, see Sanders (2006).

Chapter 4

1. These quotes are taken from email correspondence between the author and Jim Trombetta, March 17 and 19, 2008, respectively. I am grateful to him for his discussion of the show.

2. I am grateful to Aeon Skoble for discussion of the points in this paragraph.

3. Edward Barnes (1985) notes that most vice officers in Miami wore belt holsters or strapped their guns to their legs, since the kind of shoulder holsters Crockett and Tubbs are shown using required them to wear jackets, something real vice cops would find prohibitive in the Miami heat. Actual vice cops drove nondescript, low profile rental cars, not Ferraris. Perhaps the most interesting statistic is that in 1985, one episode of *Miami Vice* cost $1.3 million, a figure that exceeded the budget for the twenty-three-person vice squad for the entire year.

WORKS CITED

Abalos, Brenda. 1999. "Straightness, Whiteness, and Masculinity: Reflec- **107**
tions on *Miami Vice*." In *Race and Ideology: Language, Symbolism, and
Popular Culture*, ed. Arthur K. Spears, 167–79. Detroit: Wayne State
University Press.

Allman, T. D. 1986. *Miami: City of the Future*. New York: Atlantic Monthly
Press.

Arnett, Robert. 2006. "Eighties Noir: The Dissenting Voice in Reagan's
America." *Journal of Popular Film and Television* 34, no. 3: 127.

Barnes, Edward. 1985. "Into the Night with the Real Miami Vice." *Life*
(December): 58–66.

Benedek, Emily. 1985. "Inside *Miami Vice*." *Rolling Stone* (March 28): 56–
62, 125.

Butler, Jeremy G. 1985. "*Miami Vice:* The Legacy of *Film Noir*." *Journal of
Popular Film and Television* 13, no. 3: 127–38. Reprinted in *The Film
Noir Reader,* ed. Alain Silver and James Ursini, 289–305. New York:
Limelight Editions, 1996.

Caldwell, John. 1995. *Televisuality: Style, Crisis and Authority in American
Television*. New Brunswick, N.J.: Rutgers University Press.

DeKnock, Jan. 1985. "*Miami Vice* Makes Some Chart History." *Chicago
Tribune* (November 8): NA82.

Deroche, Constance, and John Deroche. 1991. "Black and White: Racial
Construction in Television Police Dramas." *Canadian Ethnic Studies*
23: 69–91.

Dunlop, Beth. 1989. "In *Vice* We Found Our Virtues." *Miami Herald* (May

21): 4K.

Gitlin, Todd. 1986. "Car Commercials and *Miami Vice*." In *Watching Television,* ed. Todd Gitlin, 136–61. New York: Pantheon.

Grossberg, Lawrence. 1987. "The In-Difference of Television." *Screen* 28, no. 2: 28–45.

Grossberger, Lewis. 1985. "On Location with *Miami Vice*." *TV Guide* (July 27): 26–29.

Harris, Art. 1985. "Of Vice and Mann." *Washington Post* (October 16): B1.

Hirsch, Foster. 1999. *Detours and Lost Highways: A Map of Neo-Noir.* New York: Limelight Editions.

Hoberman, J. 2007. "'A Bright, Guilty World': Daylight Ghosts and Sunshine Noir." *Artforum* (February 2007): 315–19.

Inciardi, J. A., and J. L. Dee. 1987. "From the Keystone Cops to *Miami Vice:* Images of Policing in American Popular Culture." *Journal of Popular Culture* 21, no. 2: 84–102.

Jameson, Richard T. 1985. "Men Over Miami." *Film Comment* (April 1985): 66–67.

———. 1999. "Son of *Noir*." In *The Film Noir Reader* 2, ed. Alain Silver and James Ursini, 197–205. New York: Limelight Editions.

Kellner, Douglas. 1995. *Media Culture: Cultural Studies, Identity and Politics between the Modern and Postmodern.* New York: Routledge.

King, Scott Benjamin. 1990. "Sonny's Virtues: The Gender Negotiations of *Miami Vice*." *Screen* 31, no. 3: 281–95.

Leitch, Thomas. 2002. *Crime Films.* Cambridge: Cambridge University Press.

Martin, Richard. 1997. *Mean Streets and Raging Bulls: The Legacy of Film Noir in Contemporary American Cinema.* Lanham, Md.: Scarecrow Press.

Meyer, David N. 1997. *The Best 100 Films to Rent You've Never Heard of.* New York: St. Martin's Press.

Mittel, Jason. 2004. *Genre and Television: From Cop Shows to Cartoons in American Culture.* New York: Routledge.

Moses, Michael Valdez. 2008. "Kingdom of Darkness: Autonomy and Conspiracy in *The X-Files* and *Millennium*." In *The Philosophy of TV Noir,* ed. Steven M. Sanders and Aeon J. Skoble, 203–27. Lexington: University Press of Kentucky.

O'Connor, John J. 1986a. "A Preview of NBC's 'Crime Story.'" *New York Times* (September 18): C30.

———. 1986b. "Real World Impinges on *Miami Vice*." *New York Times*

(October 19): 2:31.

Palmer, R. Barton. 1994. *Hollywood's Dark Cinema: The American Film Noir.* New York: Twayne.

———. 2008. "Dragnet, Film Noir, and Postwar Realism." In *The Philosophy of TV Noir,* ed. Steven M. Sanders and Aeon J. Skoble, 33–48. Lexington: University Press of Kentucky.

———. Forthcoming. "Steven Soderbergh and the Noir Redemption Film." In *The Philosophy of Steven Soderbergh,* ed. R. Barton Palmer and Steven M. Sanders. Lexington: University Press of Kentucky.

Porfirio, Robert. 1976. "No Way Out: Existential Motifs in the *Film Noir.*" *Sight and Sound* 45, no. 4. Reprinted in *The Film Noir Reader*, ed. Alain Silver and James Ursini. New York: Limelight Editions, 77–93, 1999.

Portes, Alejandro, and Alex Stepick. 1993. *City on the Edge: The Transformation of Miami.* Berkeley: University of California Press.

Romney, Jonathan. 1996. "Mann and His Movies." *Guardian* (London): April 18, 10.

Ross, Andrew. 1986. "Masculinity and *Miami Vice:* Selling In." *Oxford Literary Review* 8, nos. 1–2: 143–54.

Rybin, Steven. 2007. *The Cinema of Michael Mann.* Lanham, Md.: Lexington Books.

Sanders, Steven M. 2006. "Film Noir and the Meaning of Life." In *The Philosophy of Film Noir,* ed. Mark T. Conard, 91–105. Lexington: University Press of Kentucky.

Sanders, Steven M., and R. Barton Palmer, eds. 2010. *Michael Mann: Interviews.* Jackson: University Press of Mississippi.

Sanders, Steven M., and Aeon J. Skoble, eds. 2008. *The Philosophy of TV Noir.* Lexington: University Press of Kentucky.

Schmalz, Jeffrey. 1989. "Miami Journal; Sun Sets on Show That Redefined a City." *New York Times* (May 18): A1.

Scott, A. O. 2004. "Michael Mann Loves His Work." *New York Times* (August 8): 2:9.

Selby, Spencer. 1984. *Dark City: The Film Noir.* Jefferson, N.C.: McFarland.

Shales, Tom. 2002. "No Pastel-Packing 'Vice' Cops Here; 'Robbery Homicide Division' Aims True." *Washington Post* (September 27): C1.

Sharrett, Christopher. 2000. "Michael Mann's Band of Outsiders." *USA Today Magazine* 128 (March 1): 74.

Shary, Timothy. 2006. "Which Way Is Up?" *Sight & Sound* 16, no. 9: 14–18.

Skoble, Aeon J. 2006. "Moral Clarity and Practical Reason in Film Noir."

In *The Philosophy of Film Noir,* ed. Mark T. Conard, 41–49. Lexington: University Press of Kentucky.

Smith, Sally Bedell. 1985. "*Miami Vice:* Action TV with Some New Twists." *New York Times* (January 3): C20.

Sonsky, Steve. 1989. "Bye, Pal." *Miami Herald* (May 21).

Spicer, Andrew. 2002. *Film Noir.* Harlow, Eng.: Pearson Education.

Sragow, Michael. 1999. "Mann among Men." *Salon* (February 22). http://www.salon.com/bc/1999/02/02bc.html.

Telotte, J. P. 1989. *Voices in the Dark: The Narrative Patterns of Film Noir.* Urbana: University of Illinois Press.

Thompson, Kristen Moana. 2007. *Crime Films: Investigating the Scene.* London: Wallflower Press.

Thomson, David. 2004. *The New Biographical Dictionary of Film.* 4th ed., Revised and Expanded. New York: Knopf.

Trutnau, John-Paul. 2005. *A One Man Show? The Construction and Deconstruction of a Patriarchal Image in the Reagan Era: Reading the Audio-Visual Poetics of* Miami Vice. Victoria, B.C.: Trafford Publishing.

Ursini, James. 1996. "Angst at Sixty Fields per Second." In *The Film Noir Reader,* ed. Alain Silver and James Ursini, 275–87. New York: Limelight Editions.

Wang, O.N.C. 1988. "Sex, Drugs, and Rock and Roll: *Miami Vice.*" *Jump Cut* 33 (February): 10–19.

Waters, Harry F. 1985. "Pop and Cop." *Newsweek* (January 21): 67.

Wood, James. 2005. "The Blue River of Truth." *New Republic* (August 1): 24.

Wood, Michael. 2006. "At the Movies" Rev. of *Miami Vice,* dir. Michael Mann. *London Review of Books* 28, no. 16 (August 17): 14.

Zoglin, Richard. 1985. "Hot Cops, Cool Show." *Time* (September 16): 60–64.

Following the title of each episode is the episode's original broadcast date
on NBC. Four episodes from the fifth season were broadcast after the series finale.

Season One: 1984–85
 1. Pilot: Brother's Keeper: 9/16/84
 2. Heart of Darkness: 9/28/84
 3. Cool Runnin': 10/05/84
 4. Calderone's Return, Part 1: The Hit List: 10/19/84
 5. Calderone's Return, Part 2: Calderone's Demise: 10/26/84
 6. One-Eyed Jack: 11/02/84
 7. No Exit: 11/09/84
 8. The Great McCarthy: 11/16/84
 9. Glades: 11/30/84
10. Give a Little, Take a Little: 12/07/84
11. Little Prince: 12/14/84
12. Milk Run: 1/04/85
13. Golden Triangle, Part 1 (aka Score): 1/11/85
14. Golden Triangle, Part 2: 1/18/85
15. Smuggler's Blues: 2/01/85
16. Rites of Passage: 2/08/85
17. The Maze: 2/22/85
18. Made for Each Other: 3/08/85
19. The Home Invaders: 3/15/85

20. Nobody Lives Forever: 3/29/85
21. Evan: 5/03/85
22. Lombard: 5/10/85

Season Two: 1985–86
1. The Prodigal Son: 9/27/85
2. Whatever Works: 10/04/85
3. Out Where the Buses Don't Run: 10/18/85
4. The Dutch Oven: 10/25/85
5. Buddies: 11/01/85
6. Junk Love: 11/08/85
7. Tale of the Goat: 11/15/85
8. Bushido: 11/22/85
9. Bought and Paid For: 11/29/85
10. Back in the World: 12/06/85
11. Phil the Shill: 12/13/85

12. Definitely Miami: 1/10/86
13. Yankee Dollar: 1/17/86
14. One-Way Ticket: 1/24/86
15. Little Miss Dangerous: 1/31/86
16. Florence Italy: 2/14/86
17. French Twist: 2/21/86
18. The Fix: 3/07/86
19. Payback: 3/14/86
20. Free Verse: 4/04/86
21. Trust Fund Pirates: 5/02/86
22. Sons and Lovers: 5/09/86

Season Three: 1986–87
1. When Irish Eyes Are Crying: 9/26/86
2. Stone's War: 10/03/86
3. Kill Shot: 10/10/86
4. Walk Alone: 10/17/86
5. The Good Collar: 10/24/86
6. Shadow in the Dark: 10/31/86
7. El Viejo: 11/07/86
8. Better Living through Chemistry: 11/14/86
9. Baby Blues: 11/21/86
10. Streetwise 12/05/86

11. Forgive Us Our Debts: 12/12/86
12. Down for the Count, Part 1: 1/09/87
13. Down for the Count, Part 2: 1/16/87
14. Cuba Libre: 1/23/87
15. The Savage (aka Duty and Honor): 2/06/87
16. Theresa: 2/13/87
17. The Afternoon Plane: 2/20/87
18. Lend Me an Ear: 2/27/87
19. Red Tape: 3/13/87
20. By Hooker by Crook: 3/20/87
21. Knock, Knock, Who's There? 3/27/87
22. Viking Bikers from Hell: 4/03/87
23. Everybody's in Showbiz: 5/01/87
24. Heroes of the Revolution: 5/08/87

Season Four: 1987–88

 1. Contempt of Court: 9/25/87
 2. Amen . . . Send Money: 10/02/87
 3. Death and the Lady: 10/16/87
 4. The Big Thaw: 10/23/87
 5. Child's Play: 10/30/87
 6. God's Work: 11/06/87
 7. Missing Hours: 11/13/87
 8. Like a Hurricane: 11/20/87
 9. Rising Sun of Death: 12/04/87
10. Love at First Sight: 1/15/88
11. A Rock and a Hard Place: 1/22/88
12. The Cows of October: 2/05/88
13. Vote of Confidence: 2/12/88
14. Baseballs of Death: 2/19/88
15. Indian Wars: 2/26/88
16. Honor among Thieves? 3/04/88
17. Hell Hath No Fury: 3/11/8
18. Badge of Dishonor: 3/18/88
19. Blood and Roses: 4/01/88
20. A Bullet for Crockett: 4/15/88
21. Deliver Us from Evil: 4/29/88
22. Mirror Image: 5/06/88

Season Five: 1988–89

1. Hostile Takeover: 11/04/88
2. Redemption in Blood: 11/11/88
3. Heart of Night: 11/18/88
4. Bad Timing: 12/02/88
5. Borrasca: 12/09/88
6. Line of Fire: 12/16/88
7. Asian Cut: 1/13/89
8. Hard Knocks: 1/20/89
9. Fruit of the Poison Tree: 2/03/89
10. To Have and to Hold: 2/10/89
11. Miami Squeeze: 2/17/89
12. Jack of All Trades: 3/03/89
13. The Cell Within: 3/10/89
14. The Last Madonna: 3/17/89
15. Over the Line: 4/28/89

16. Victims of Circumstance: 5/05/89
17. Freefall (Series Finale): 5/12/89
18. World of Trouble: 6/14/89
19. Miracle Man: 6/21/89
20. Leap of Faith: 6/28/89
21. Too Much, Too Late: 1/25/90

Episodes of *Miami Vice* are in quotation marks, as are titles of songs (with parenthetical references to their performers). References to Don Johnson and Philip Michael Thomas, which can be found on nearly every page of this book, are too numerous to list. Fictional characters other than Sonny Crockett and Ricardo Tubbs who play an important role in the book's discussion are indexed under the name of the actor portraying them.